Staying Alive
SURVIVING SURPRISES

by Joan Peet Milner

Staying Alive: Surviving Surprises (A Memoir)
Published in the USA by
Joan Peet Milner aka 2dogs Publishing
554 East Magee Road
Tucson, Arizona 85704 USA
2dogspubs@gmail.com

Library of Congress Cataloging-in-Publication Data
Milner, Joan P. writer
Staying Alive: A Memoir
LCCN: 2025906755
Subjects: LCSH, memoir

Paperback ISBN: 97921859158 8
eBook ISBN: 979821864900 5
PDF ISBN: 979821864901 2

Book Design by Brooke O'Neill (United Fulfillment)
Cover photo by Ron Clark (Harbour Master, Calabar) with repair by Tim Miller (Great Projections, Tucson), and Marnie Sharp.
Photograph: Joan and Allison in Ikpai, Biafra 1968

These are true stories. Family details in Breaking the Law story have been slightly changed.

Donations from sales of this book will be given to
Special Needs Solutions in Tucson, AZ.

For Roger, the curious adventurer;
and for Mark, the scientific explorer.

In Memory of our dear friend and
neighbour, Deborah (Debi) Rae Donegan.

Praise for Staying Alive

Through seemingly impulsive responces to intriguing and frightening situations, Joan Peet Milner describes a life few of us can imagine. This quiet British young woman faced situations we usually only read about in novels, but this was her life. And she stayed alive through it all. In enchanting prose, we travel with her to the souks of Jeddah, the refugee camps and hospitals of Biafra, in the 1960s. A must read.

Elizabeth Leah Reed, writer and author of Mrs Musterman, Miliner of Main Street. A Biography

---

What a beautifully expressed recounting of one woman's path through a very difficult set of circumstances.

Sarah Fehlig, St Louis, Missouri USA

What surprised me about the author, was how much she went with the flow at the time, following a man through amazing adventures across the world. It is a remarkable story of travel, countries, crises and cultures. But it's also a story of a young British occupational therapist taking a chance on a man and trusting him as he went about his international endeavors both overt and secretive -and how she reflects on it all with hindsight.

Lesley Kerr-Edwards, Educator, High Wycombe, UK

This adventurous and passion-filled true story by Joan Peet Milner takes the reader on journeys that start in the 1940s in war-torn England, on to the mysterious souks of

Morocco and into the heart of darkness of deepest Africa in the 1960s and 70s. Her tales of Saudi Arabia and Nigeria are mesmerizing. Her story includes flights in war birds in dangerous places, a pilot husband, and accounts of her life-threatening close encounters of all kinds. Through it all, Joan survives the risks, endures the pain, and stays alive. Once you start reading this you will not be able to put it down.

Jon Vick, Author and Captain USAF, Valley Center, California.

True stories by an ordinary woman who did extraordinary things.

Nan Abrams, Author of Bret Harte, Scribe of Uniontown, Humboldt County, CA   Available in Humboldt County Library.

These amazing adventures around the world are captivating. I'm glad they are in print because it is a fascinating and unique odyssey. The details about the author's animal friends and human friends in Africa interspersed with the horrors and challenges of the Biafran war give us an intimate experience of her daily life despite the large events all around. Describing efforts to try to live a freer and more satisfying life within the rigid social rules of Saudi Arabia is very effective in painting a picture of what it was like for her as a woman in that country, showing her personal growth.

Pamela Park, Librarian, Tucson, Arizona.

CONTENTS

PREFACE

Lucky Me

As a baby in an elegant British pram, I ended up on the railroad tracks at Sheffield's busy Midland Station. My mother had left me outside the platform travel office while she went in to buy tickets for us to take the train to visit my grandparents in the north of England. Rushing, because the train was due to arrive, she hadn't adequately secured the pram's brakes, which allowed it to spontaneously start rolling across the slightly sloping platform. When she exited with the tickets, the pram had disappeared. It had nosedived onto the tracks about three to four feet below the platform the mattress sliding during the fall, protected my head. My loud indignant cries alerted my mother and the station staff to my invisible location. After giving each other a 'shall we' look, two platform guards put their own lives at risk by quickly running, jumping down to the tracks and carefully lifting my pram back to the platform. Within minutes the huge north bound train screeched into the station, its steam engine puffing out thick black smoke.

My first escape.

Lucky me seems to be a common thread running through these stories. I cannot consciously recall that first incident, it's only by having heard the story as a child that it remains a memory and there is no one left of the Sheffield family to corroborate its validity.

In 2013, I experienced another threat, this time from a brush with a cancer that came rushing into my life like a demon train. Since I'd been thinking vaguely about writing the stories I'd told to many friends over time, often met with an enthusiastic 'you should write these down.' I realized I'd better get started. But how to start, which stories to tell, when and where to begin? I hadn't a clue.

I needed help to organize my thoughts. What I wanted to tell were stories about life with a man into whose trap I fell within hours of our meeting, and the long, gradual downhill slide with joy and adventures, obstacles and secrets, that ended in divorce twenty years later.

In 2014, while absentmindedly skimming through a catalog of classes that had come in the mail, out popped 'Memoir Writing' (8 weeks). Picking up the phone to register was as fast as a knee jerk. It was serendipity. With the stories constantly bubbling up in my head, well known teacher Molly McKasson, provided me a way to tap into them. After the eighth class I decided to jump into writing with the joy and surprise Molly had promised. I share these stories of mine, as a sort of memoir, a collection of individual experiences that came my way while living with Terry Peet in Nigeria and Saudi Arabia from 1968 to 1983.

These are true stories.

PART ONE

Early Memories

1

A Four-Year-Old's War Story

I had known war as a very young child in England, living on the outskirts of Sheffield, a large industrial center in the Midlands. In the evenings when the haunting air raid siren signaled German planes approaching to bomb the factories along the Don River, facilities that, in earlier times, had canned peas and made Licorice Allsorts sweets, my mother, with her shaky heart, joined the Langsett Avenue housewives and went into action. Their mission was to protect those substantial buildings, which, by 1939, had been converted to making munitions. The fewer bombs in the British arsenal the happier the Germans would be. Consequently, those buildings were important enemy targets.

They were in the valley a mile or so from our home up a steep residential hill that stretched from the river bottom. With all the men away in uniform somewhere, the most able-bodied women in the village were organized to do what they could to protect the factories. I recently learned that I had an uncle who, unable to join the army because of some infirmity, became an Air Raid Precautions Warden and served his country by organizing the local defense team of which my mother was a volunteer.

On a moonless night, when an eerie siren wail filled the air, the neighbours grabbed a blanket or two, jumped into their Wellington boots and climbed over garden walls. They ran down the springtime bluebell-covered hillside, dodging rocks and trees, across the cricket pitch, down into the valley. All the while, they listened for the drone of engines and watched, watched for ejected incendiary bombs from German planes that would illuminate targets as they fell, providing light for approaching bombers. Once on the ground the ladies ran to smother them with their blankets to both prevent the spread of fire and return the valley to the safety of darkness. Not one factory on the river was ever hit. But the city of Sheffield, three miles to the southeast, with its concentration of steel mills and weapons manufacturing, was wrecked, many parts totally flattened, thousands of homes destroyed, and hundreds of residents killed.

Every home, every building in England had to use 'blackout' during every night of the war. It was Mr. Churchill's idea to have every window covered with heavy black curtains at dusk. If German planes flew over England during daylight, they became easy targets. Flying at night gave some protection but with no identifiable landmarks the pilots' attempts to locate important targets were frustrated by the endless darkness (radar wasn't widely used until after the war). The women, therefore, had to get to the fiery light sources as quickly as possible. It was dangerous hard work for housewives who, till then, were not particularly physically fit. Their dedication was successful: the Don Valley factories were protected and still remain intact beside the river.

However, that effort contributed to my mother's early demise at age fifty-three, during my 21st year, her body, damaged by childhood rheumatic fever, never recovered from the exertion required to run up and down the hills. In spite of her fragile heart, she never refused to do her part.

For the first four years of my life, whenever there was an air raid on Sheffield, as my mother grabbed her blankets and boots, she grabbed me, too, and ran with her precious bundle to the air raid shelter at the bottom of our garden. There, grandmotherly neighbour Mrs. Taylor, too old to join the lady firefighters, would be at the door to our underground bunker, opening it up. With other local children, I spent the night, or as much of it as necessary, with Granny Taylor and her lavender scented hankies, sleeping on one of the narrow benches that ran from front to back like seats in an army troop transport. I remember the shelter's ceiling, long and low; its damp earthy smell;

the rows of pegs on which hung gas masks of various sizes; the rubbery smell of the mask when I tried it on, fitting closely over my face, stretching my eyes; and that terrible, eerie siren. If I hear that sound now in a movie or as an earthquake warning, it still makes me freeze in fear.

Once the Armistice was declared, the good news spread quickly though our village that the soldiers, sailors and pilots were coming home[1]. I overheard Sylvia, my mother and the aunties making excited plans to welcome my father, Joseph, home, but with no memory of ever having met my father, I felt apprehension rather than jubilation. I remember the special day as a whirl of activity. My mother was on the move, unable to be still, looking out of the small stained-glass window in the front door where a shadow of movement signaled someone walking along the passage to the kitchen door everyone used.

By noon no one had arrived. We had lunch. I suspect family members living nearby were being distant so my dad could have some private time with his family before his brothers and sisters, unable to resist, would call around to welcome him home too. But he didn't come during daylight hours. Still in my pretty dress sewn by Mum especially for the occasion, I had my dinner and eventually,

---

1 For the duration of WWII my father, Joseph Milner, served as ship's secretary on the Royal Navy's lead battleship: King George V.

with reluctance on my mother's part, we climbed upstairs for my bath in preparation for bed.

Feelings of disappointment permeated the bathroom, even though Mum did her best to be lighthearted as usual. Then we heard heavy footsteps on the stairs. The door squeaked open. Mum, on her knees, hung over the edge of the bath, a sponge in her hand, and with a few loose strands of hair across her face, was reminded that this was not how she had planned to greet her husband. She turned and looked up. I did too.

There stood a tall, uniformed man, his wide smile framed by a black mustache and beard. He stood with his arms open in my bathroom, and I, naked in the bath. Horrified and with nowhere to hide, I made myself into a hedgehog-like ball, turned my back, hid my face and cried out, 'Take him away.'

My dad, of course, relieved to be home, hadn't realized how limited my experience was with men in general. Neither parent had anticipated my reaction, but they rallied to placate me with calming whispers and reassured each other that this would pass. I don't recall getting into pajamas, being comforted and tucked into bed with, I suppose, a kiss from Mum and an unwelcomed, hairy snuggle from Dad. With so much love between them, inevitably I was infected by it. It only took a week or two because during subsequent days, as men returned to their homes, they were everywhere. My friends, the girls and boys of Langsett Avenue, played cricket in the road with their dads, dads walked with their children along trails over the Common. They waited in line at the grocers, men drove cars, worked on buses, in gardens. Dads in church.

And as the days passed, both mum and dad were doing all those things with me. My father's presence and obvious delight in being with his wife and little girl slowly filled my life with happy security in spite of that disastrous introduction.

These early perils of war were etched in my young memory as a one time experience but life had other plans for me on another continent far away.

A Seven Year Old's Poem

My mother, born a Geordie, in the north east corner of England close to the Scottish border, whose accents are known to be the most gentle and lilting in all of England, was not happy, I couldn't help developing a Yorkshire accent, living and playing with neighbour children in my home of Wadsley village, just west of Sheffield in the Midlands. The accent the neighbour children used was identified as 'working class' then. Mum loved the home she had left and without being snobbish, she wanted me to grow up speaking with a neutral voice, which meant elocution lessons.

Classes started during the summer of 1948 when I was seven years old, with the learning of this poem for a class competition. I enjoyed the imagery so much it has stayed with me all these seventy-seven years. Though its title and ending are lost, the sentiments it suggests might have inspired me to ...adventure.

If ever I travel to France or Spain.
I mean to go in an aeroplane
I've read all about it and now I know
How they swing the propellers and off you go.

A run and a bounce and you're soon looking down
From high in the sky on a little toy town.
With fields like a bedspread green and brown
With ribbony roads all winding through.
So empty and quiet it hardly seems true
That they're looking up to see you
Racing along like a big letter T
Through the clouds and into the light,
Smaller and smaller, and out of sight.
And next you're abroad, and I hope it seems

Just as lovely as in your dreams;
With castles, cathedrals, cities with walls,
Forests and fountains and waterfalls.
Great grim mountains all rocks and snow
And broad bright rivers away below.

So, if ever I travel to France or Spain,
I mean to go in an aeroplane.

I won.

2

Minitreck to Morocco

From Fes, Morocco, we drove south in bright sunshine, just as the brochures had promised us: six young adult adventurers from five different countries, stuck together in the confines of a tiny bus. I was nineteen years old. For miles and miles, day after day, we waited for the moment when we'd be let out to stretch, breathe fresh air, fill our minds with whatever was new at the place where we'd spend that night. Now the sky was ominously dark, heavy with low rumbling, grey clouds and determined winds that bounced off the High Atlas Mountains onto our worn, blue VW Minivan, pushing us this way and that in a crazy slalom along the narrow desert road, challenging Dave, our driver. We were so small compared to the massive mountains. But there was no rain, not yet, that's why Dave was so merciless on the accelerator. We had to get to Marrakesh before the rain, or chance being swept off the road.

We traveled from London, heading through France, to our destination: Morocco, on the north-west corner of the continent of Africa. *Minitrek Expeditions* were all the rage in the early 1960s. Their adventures were well organized providing for middle class young adults just the right amount of free time, independence, protection, and opportunity. Treks went in all directions around the world, even as far as India, Australia. The one I had chosen was relatively short in miles but vast in cultural shock. I would be leaving the safe, familiar comfort of my old English and relatively new Canadian homes to visit a country where everything would be strange, and I was ready. There was no real danger. Dave had successfully made the trip many times.

A ferry ride across the English Channel followed by a short drive through northern France found us in Rouen, where we arrived in time for a late supper of *moules et frites*, a delicious French welcome. I'll never forget being awoken that first morning in Rouen's ancient center as loud bells clanged close by; the smell of baking bread drifted through the open dormer window. It was early in the still dark, snug, top floor room of the *pension*. I'd been dragged out of my narrow bed by the dominating presence of the 12th century Cathedral of Rouen. The narrow, cobbled street, shiny from a recent rain, was empty as I followed those bells and smells, shivering in the damp morning air, to a most extraordinary and unexpected experience.

The church door was old, wooden, deeply carved, and heavy to pull open just enough to slide around. Were there lights inside? Incense! Then a couple of candles flickered far away, they too beckoned me. I had to reach for the solid old pews as if I were blind to quietly make my way towards the unsteady lights. As I got closer, I realized there were four figures cloaked in black huddled together on the front bench to the left of the nave. I had chosen the same aisle as they had to reach the candles.

Settling in behind the people I sat enthralled by the feeling this building gave me, its gentle embrace, as if the air could caress with texture, no, with energy of soft substance. We were enveloped in sweet smelling darkness.

A clear, pure, young voice broke the silence, singing a prayer in Latin, not French, a prayer I didn't understand but knew I wanted to let fall all over me to fill my empty spaces, the ones I didn't even know about. So I closed my eyes and entered a reverie of fragrance, of people close by, of a choir boy somewhere. Time passed softly. When the priest started to speak in accented French, I was startled to understand. He read from: 1 Corinthians, Chapter 13, 'Though I speak with the tongues of men and of angels and have not charity...,' I had learned that whole passage for my Confirmation when I was twelve years old. I felt a flutter of recognition and a small smile of welcome.

When I opened my eyes, another surprise filled me. Behind the now vaguely visible altar a huge pink circle of stained glass was materializing, its breadth and height seemed impossible. How could there be walls and roof to accommodate this enormous window which, as the seconds ticked by, became a brilliant roseate, mesmerizing spectacle? As the rising sun continued to fill Rouen Cathedral's glorious rose window with colour, I knew it was a spiritual gift of self-reliance I would treasure throughout my life.

I have so often thought about how, eight hundred years ago under the most grueling of physical and doctrinal circumstances, the great cathedral of Rouen had been built with this important feature. Many other large, leaded glass windows, both circular and elongated, were incorporated into the building's structure, each capturing the magic of sunshine to create daily inspiration. A dramatic Medieval argument for the power of God.

Our trek continued south to Spain where other delights satisfied my curiosity: passionate flamenco guitars; dramatic, feisty flamenco dances; that plaintive flamenco song half-cry, half- howl. The beauty of tiled and intricately carved Alhambra with its cool, peaceful courtyards, so different from the old palaces, churches, and castles of

England. Most English people did not gather for supper at midnight to eat paella in noisy outdoor cafes.

And the Guardia Civil. We had a run-in with General Franco's elite guards whose frightening authority gave them the reputation of 'shooting first and asking questions later.' We were stopped at a passport checkpoint where our New Zealand bus mate's papers were questioned. The Guardia, a really rough bunch with their squared off, shiny, black helmets, took us into a smelly anteroom in their station and made us all feel guilty with their threatening gestures as they spat out rapid Spanish. They roughly searched through the New Zealander's passport and backpack while giving us threatening looks across a cigarette burnt table, holding my breath, my light-heartedness disappeared. Eventually we were paraded outside to wait in the shade, grey clouds of fear surrounding us; I used the calming rose window to ease my worried mind.

After that disturbing scare and a two-hour delay, the questioned passport was returned, and we continued to Gibraltar. Its 'Barbary apes' (Macaque monkeys) were on duty at the peak, teasing us for food. Looking across the Mediterranean at the Straits of Gibraltar and down on the docks where the ferry was moored, we could see our transportation and destination: Ceuta, Morocco, Africa. Within the following weeks we discovered Tangier, Rabat,

Casablanca, Fes, and eventually Marrakesh, where we finally arrived before the torrential rains.

Learning to speak French was a given while living as a teenager in *Montréal*, but I had no previous knowledge of Morocco's Arabic language, customs, writing, food; its music, art, and architecture. All were completely foreign and wonderfully intriguing. I was so fascinated by things Moroccan that I took to exploring on my own whenever Dave gave the OK.

But as it turned out, that wasn't the best idea. Fate and the unknown future traveled with me as my wanderlust grew in complexity. Childhood in rural Yorkshire with freedom to explore beyond my village had built in me an ability to react quickly, Wiley Coyote style. I had carried that ability with me through my nineteen years, although I didn't realize its value until the following stories percolated into memory; and as I recalled them, I realized how resilient I had become to life's challenges.

3

Gallantry

I met the man on a ferry.

I was in a hurry when I descended the stairs into the bar, to settle in for a good read with a beer as the boat would gently rock me across the English Channel to Belgium. The man politely stood and offered me the chair beside him, the only one available in the room. As I sat down he helped me scoot closer to the table and introduced himself. He was Terry, that's all I knew.

My home was in *Montréal.* I'd been visiting family in England during my summer vacation of 1965. I was twenty four and heading to Europe again to follow my whims with a skeleton itinerary anchored to reservations at youth hostels. I would hitch my way from Belgium to Luxembourg then into the Black Forest of Germany, taking each day to savour foods and wines, read and hike and explore for a lazy, self-indulgent couple of weeks. But the unexpected gallantry changed all that.

We talked our way to Ostend over beer and Ayn Rand's *'Atlas Shrugged'* and continued traveling together by train to Brugge, and on to Brussels. The youth hostel I'd booked for the night had just closed when we approached its door at 10:00 pm. No-one answered my persistent knock. So what to do? Terry seemed determined to stay with me, taking charge by asking a patrolling policeman where the nearest hotel might be. A quick walk away and there it was. Within minutes we were together in the last available double-bedded room. There was sex, a kind of desperate conviction on his part that there would be. It wasn't rape. I didn't fight. It was as if I was a compassionate observer of myself, aware and concerned about precautions and curious too. He assured me he had precautions but there was no sign of any I recognized in the morning light. I was amazed, not traumatized, that such a thing could happen to me. Had I fallen for the gallantry that had turned to opportunism?

Or had I tuned in to his tortured soul because many years later he told me the sad story about what he'd done earlier that day: to escape an empty marriage and a stunted working situation he had abandoned wife and two young daughters by staging his own death by drowning. To fulfill his dream he was going to Africa where he could do good works saving civilians in war torn southern Congo. But that wasn't the whole story.

Through days of increasing intimacy, we shared a room at *Hotel La Ruche*, across from Brussel's *Gare du Nord* train station in the city center. The manager invited us to join her and her regulars at the family table where evening meals were served in a back corner of the spacious dining room. It was Terry who made an immediate connection with a slim, short, wiry middle-aged South African called Oscar and his girlfriend Fabiola (not her real name we found out) as we ate together in the dark. Oscar had lived in the Congo about which he told numerous stories including how his left foot was blown off by a landmine. He used a crutch to get around. He was a gangster, commando, smuggler, an alien without a passport with a wallet full of 1000-franc notes, and a gun. One night after a communal supper of *moules, frites* and beer, Oscar casually poured the contents of a well-worn leather pouch onto the table midst the empty dishes. As one small stone rolled onto the floor, I stooped to find it. Oscar told me not to bother, the maid would sweep it up later and never know it was an uncut diamond! As a gunrunner and a rascal, his preferred currency was those innocent little rocks. Terry was impressed.

We accepted Oscar's invitation to join him and Fabiola on a quick, hair-raising ride to Alsace and back in the smuggler's red Thunderbird convertible with automatic transmission he could drive with one foot, stopping only to drink beer and eat *pommes frites* along the way. The girlfriend and I sat recklessly on top of the folded roof, our hair and clothes whipped by the exhilarating speed.

Every weekday morning, Terry left the hotel soon after a quick breakfast of bread, cheese and black coffee and because I wanted to escape the bizarre and sometimes scary influence of Oscar and Fabiola, I became the tourist I'd planned on being in Brussels. The World Fair site, Expo '58, was an early discovery: an intriguing remnant of a world within a world. Its international pavilions of mirrored glass and its Atomium, a large metal replica of an iron atom which became Brussels' icon, were surrounded by park-like flower gardens outlined by paths. I'd often return to wander there in quiet solitude or have lunch and a read in the restaurant at the apex of the Atomium. My visits to that site with its flowers and history of unique buildings once staffed by people from countries the world over, inspired me to become a Hostess at the British Pavilion at *Montréal's* Expo: 'Man and His World,' the 1967 World's Fair.

The Grande Place in Brussels' city center became another favourite destination during my days alone. I loved its vestiges of tall medieval Guild Hall buildings. There, quaint *cafés* whose rich aromas of roasted coffee beans and vanilla cakes met me at their doors with invitations to 'come in,' I confess to enjoying many cups of strong coffee and sweet hot chocolate. Those weekday saunters around the Grande Place without the noisy weekend distractions slowed me down. I would sit on a sunny bench with a book and camera, taking in metaphors of grandness. Often, when local people and tourists, complete strangers, joined me for a chat, I began to realize how my rattly *Québécois* accent, was softening. I was developing an ear for the richness of real French.

On Sundays, a flower market filled the vast space with a rainbow of colours, and a bouquet of fragrance from thousands of exotic and familiar blossoms. Terry and I would meander through a labyrinth of flower filled buckets, sit on the market's periphery and just inhale its intensity.

Each visit to the Grande Place included a stop at *Mannekin Pis*, the statue of the little boy whose wartime activities contributed to Brussels' pride and resilient spirit. We'd give his shiny brass arm an affectionate rub.

I had been traveling to Europe since my university days, but this experience had a new spiciness to it. I was enjoying a relationship with a man five years my senior and completely different to any previous male friends. He seemed to be as happy with me as I was with him, hobnobbing around

Brussels' city center in trendy bars and restaurants. I felt my life take on a new dimension of maturity. And possibility.

———

It was not coincidence that Oscar had a Congolese connection with La Ruche. The hotel was supported by men seeking their fortunes in that African country, as I discovered when, after several days of this Bohemian lifestyle, Terry casually mentioned in his 'Oh, by the way' manner, that the following day he too would be leaving for the Congo. The Congo? Why hadn't I made the link between the Congo and Belgium? Oh, the Congo. Stunned and stumbling with nowhere to put my body, I sat down hard on my backpack.

That night, the eve of his departure, he finally told me: his reason for being in Brussels was to have had interviews at the Congolese Embassy and, if accepted, sign a contract to fly helicopters in that country. Arrangements had been made while I had been exploring or blissfully window shopping. Why hadn't he told me that earlier? The happy *ménage* was suddenly going to end.

He left by a morning train from Brussels' bustling *Gare du Nord*. With no spring in my steps, I walked with him across the busy main road to the station, making our way through commuter crowds hurrying to trains. To find the right platform he checked huge schedules whose constant departure times, destinations, and platform updates noisily flipped overhead like a shuffled pack of cards. When the clattering stopped and he found the platform he needed, I waved goodbye. He was excited and gone, leaving me feeling redundant. Fabiola and the smuggler had also left town. I was alone.

Along those paths we'd traveled at the World Fair site I took many lonely walks, my feet leaden, my gaze downcast. From the benches where I'd sat with him without giving a thought to how little I knew about him, I wrote letters. Naive and trusting, I had believed what he expressed so ardently, that his intention was to go to the Congo and do something bold and useful with his life.

His departure had happened quickly, without time for any discussion, no wonder I felt I'd been left in the dust. As it turned out, he wrote copious letters, nurtured our relationship and instead of seeing this experience as a warning, the love I felt would motivate me to be loyal to him for years.

4

An Invitation to Nigeria

My 1965 summer holiday was over, but it had been monumental; I had met a man, a gentleman, so riveting and exciting he had captured my heart almost instantly. Was it possible? What little I knew about him was hardly significant: he wanted fly helicopters to save lives in the Congo where a civil war was playing out in the south of that huge country. That was it?

I'd returned to *Montréal* and work as an occupational therapist at the Royal Victoria Hospital, while continuing my correspondence with Terry. The months passed. His letters were loving, and I believed them. He told me what he wanted me to know: where he was flying, how many nuns he'd rescued, how he had escaped when his helicopter suddenly lost altitude. It was compelling and exciting reading. I even heard about other women in his life, young employees in the US Foreign Office he would meet at parties in Kinshasa. None of that concerned me, for, although he was partying with others, he was still writing to me. My feelings were secure.

Then in early 1967, the *Montréal Star* newspaper reported progress of the World's Fair site taking shape on *Ile St Hélène*, one of *Montréal's* park-like green islands in the St Lawrence River and ran advertisements looking for staff. Scheduled to open in early summer, it was what I'd been waiting for. As a British citizen living in Canada, I hurriedly applied to be a hostess at my country's Pavilion and was granted an interview during which, by knowing what a truncheon was, (a heavy, solid club used by British Bobbies, police men) I was accepted. My hospital employer kindly gave me six months' leave of absence. Mini-skirted in red, white, and blue with a Union Jack shoulder bag and umbrella and a blue beret, we British hostesses were a colourful, classy group.

The fair was a world of activity when Terry surprised me with the prospect of a visit. A note arrived from Kinshasa: he had business in *Montréal* so could we spend a couple of weeks together and perhaps, visit the fair? Once he arrived, he charmed my roommates and moved into our little apartment. It was during this visit that he had meetings with 'Call-Me-Geoff Gould.' Meetings he brushed off as insignificant; a reference I didn't pay much attention to, being more amused by the name Terry gave him than any *raison d'etre*. However, many years later the real significance of those meetings would undo me in a devastating way when I learned what his business in *Montréal* was really about.

—————

Being a Hostess at the British Pavilion meant dealing with all the thousands of public visitors: from greeting them at reception, putting a gold stamp in their Fair-passports, to escorting dignitaries around the exhibits. On the day Terry arrived, I had spent the afternoon with Princess Margaret, answering her questions and chatting about the enormous gleaming Rolls Royce engine of Concorde fame as Beatles' songs serenaded us in the distance. The day before, I'd been assigned to stand at the top of the very long escalator as Haile Selassie, Ethiopia's Lion of Judah, rode up alone, in terror, clutching both hand rails. When the worst happened and the escalator suddenly stopped I saw the desperate pleading look in his eyes. I, in spite of having been told not to touch his majesty, was about to run towards the panic-stricken man when one of his body guards pushed me aside and held the king in a bear-hug till the problem was remedied, but I held his frightened eyes.

So many memories.

Before leaving to return to the Congo, Terry invited me to visit him in Kinshasa for a two-week holiday. Kinshasa! How could I refuse? I had crisscrossed from north to south through Morocco in1960 but Africa the continent, was mysterious. This was an invitation I couldn't resist. I would go the following summer.

Situations in Africa can quickly change. Whims of politicians swing hot and cold and power, once solid and predictable, could become threatening. From Kinshasa, year-end letters I received daily, started to contain hints of caution. Continuing to fly for the Congo's President Mobutu and traveling on his presidential yacht, Terry was close enough to hear rumours that tensions were increasing and security in Kinshasa deteriorating. He started to look for somewhere safer to fly by putting the word out to his pilot friends that he needed to leave the Congo. As had frequently happened in the past, he was invited to join them, this time in Lagos, Nigeria, where the Biafran civil war created opportunities for airmen. It was typical of Terry's spontaneous problem-solving that something always turned up.

Which meant I would start my African holiday in Lagos, the following January 1968.

PART TWO

Silent Drums

5

The Time Had Come

By the end of 1967 my relationship with Terry had deepened with his frequent visits to *Montréal* during the intervening years, he understood my infatuation with travel to distant places.

I had accepted his invitation to visit him in Lagos, Nigeria, without having any idea what to expect. It was a leap of faith and the beginning of adventures far beyond those I'd enjoyed traveling alone, hitching and youth hosteling around Europe every summer since I'd started to earn a living in1962. I'd traveled back and forth across the Atlantic from *Montréal* to London and Southampton several times either by Trans Canada Airlines DC-8; Pan Am's Super Continental Boeing 707; Cunard Line and P&O ships, too, but hadn't ventured farther than Europe and Morocco. Nigeria was definitely farther.

Once I felt those silent drums summoning me, I hustled to put my home behind me, but for how long? Since I really didn't know when I'd return, I resigned from the Royal Victoria Hospital OT Department, sold my funky old

Pontiac, emptied my room in the apartment shared with my two flatmates, said goodbye to my young brother Peter, my dad and his wife Ella, and to all my friends. Year-end parties had been tinged with blended anticipation and sadness. Was I crazy? It was a big step.

———

With my passport up to date and well hidden with some Canadian dollars and the Pam Am tickets Terry had sent from Nigeria, I was prepared for my departure on 2nd January 1968, to travel to Lagos, Nigeria. This was going to be a long series of four flights, the first of which would take me to New York's JFK Airport. My instructions included to look for Dr. Close, personal physician to the Congo's President Mobutu. Both the doctor and his daughter, famous American actress Clenn Close, were good friends of Terry's. And because I would be traveling on the same flight as the doctor across the Atlantic, Terry hinted that he'd arranged for us to travel together, at least part way.

Not one to miss an opportunity, I used the four-hour layover in New York to take the train into the city to do a little shopping at Lord and Taylor's. Looking for summery clothes in wintry *Montréal* had been disappointing, I had to find a lightweight dress, and I did. The perfect all-purpose item was knitted of a blended mix of fine linen and silk threads in modest autumn colours: a smart shirtwaist that had long sleeves, high color, buttons down the front, a straight skirt with pockets, that ended just above the knees. I could scrunch it into my handbag. It was everything I needed to travel in Africa, or so I thought.

I got back to the airport with plenty of time to check-in at economy for my flight to Lagos and search for Dr. Close but my inquiries at the First-Class desk were unproductive. I would be traveling alone.

In my diary I noted an uneventful Pan AM flight. Before the plane even took off, we in the back, were presented with an elaborately decorated menu to study. Just reading it created a mood of relaxation and comfort, a suggestion to 'sit back and enjoy' since it was going to be a long, long flight. I remember thinking that if I was going to sample all the wonderful food and drink offerings, I would have to stay in the air for a week. This was better than the Ritz Carlton. Choices included Cocktails, Canapes, Cornish Game Hen. I kicked off my shoes and sat back watching the glitter of the city fade into greyness. What pleasure.

Soon the cabin became alive with activity. They were called 'stewardesses' at the time: qualified nurses wearing smart pale blue suits with matching 'pill box' hats and high heeled shoes. They started to deliver rectangular grey trays covered with a little white cotton cloth and a cloth napkin, real cutlery, real glassware. Then the decisions started: 'Something to drink?' I requested a Manhattan. My father's favourite cocktail had become mine too. I wish I could remember which canapes arrived followed by which wine and entree, but the flights were long and attention from those caring suited ladies was constant. All the time, the plump lady missionary beside me gently snored.

We flew across the Atlantic under darkening skies, landed in Senegal, Dakar, where I had my first breath of hot, thick African air while walking on African earth in the middle of a clear starry night. The next stop was Robert's Field, Monrovia, then on to Accra, Ghana, which likely was where Dr. Close transferred to his Kinshasa flight, capital of the Republic of Congo [1].

But landing gear problems in Accra and some hold up with customs delayed our continuation, so I arrived at Ikeja Airport in Lagos, several hours late, in the afternoon of fourth January 1968.

In retrospect, that flying marathon with landings at three west African countries prepared me for what happened

---

1 President Mobuto changed his country's name to Zaire in 1971 and Laurent Kabila changed it back to Democratic Republic of Congo when he became president in 1997.

next by giving me a dose of their airport chaos. The Nigerian sweltering heat and humidity were therefore not surprises.

Walking across the blistered tarmac, this time to Nigerian Immigration and Customs, all bright lights, congestion, and freezing air conditioning were not surprising either. The grey-white walled corridor narrowed, and I was swept along with the swarm of excited disembarking passengers through narrow spaces between tables lined with uniformed officers who asked the usual questions: 'Where are you going?' and 'What is the purpose of your visit?' Still no surprise. Until a uniformed lady grabbed my sleeve and asked me in a twangy accent I would quickly learn to understand, 'What are you bringing into the country?' The vagueness of the question confused me, did she want me to list the contents of my backpack? Having snatched my passport, she tugged me behind a curtain hung across a corner of the room that created a small, private space where she proceeded, without warning, to pat me down: arm pits, under my breasts, pockets, waist, then up between my legs and down to my feet. Finding her explorations devoid of booty, she let me rearrange my clothes, pulled back the curtain, ripped a corner off a well-thumbed, folded newspaper on which she wrote 'OK,' stuck it in my passport, and gestured how to get to baggage claim. That search. That was the real surprise.

I walked out of the chill into sticky heat fuming with humiliation. In retrospect, when I understood that Nigeria was a country at war, I could rationalize that wartime demanded extreme measures by Immigration officials. They would be part of Nigeria's defense. However, there was no time to react. Realizing that I was trembling, I found and grabbed my heavy backpack and allowed myself to be jostled outside to mingle with the hot, smelly crowd of celebrating, noisy Nigerians.

Among the multitude of smiling black faces, I eagerly searched for a familiar white face without success. There was, however, a small clutch of four white faces, one of which I recognized as Charlie, a friend of Terry's from Kinshasa, I'd seen him in photos. He was there to meet me with other pilot friends. There had been no warning from Terry to prepare me. No, 'Oh, by the way, you'll be met by Charlie and friends.'

Disappointment made me somewhat subdued, but the relief at being safe and no longer alone was enormous as we walked in a close group across the crowded road to the parking lot, someone carrying my backpack. All of them were like mother hens jabbering on, trying to make up for Terry's absence. Explaining that he would be in Lagos the following day, they took me 'home' to the Federal Palace Airport Hotel in Ikeja where, after forty-eight hours of traveling, a meal, and a shower, I slept till the next afternoon.

6

An African Education

What had I done to incur this surprising imprisonment? If only there wasn't the smell.

I had no idea what my future held. Was I hostage or prisoner for life or just for an hour or two? Were my recent donations to the new Amnesty International going to pay off, for me? I tried to inhibit these irrational ideas by tuning in to the rose window of Rouen Cathedral and monitoring my breathing: slowly in, slowly out.

⁓

Only three days after my arrival in Lagos from *Montréal*, Terry, having some urgent business to attend to, flew alone, directly to Kinshasa. Why couldn't I have traveled with him? Instead, I would join him two days later by taking a different route. Although aware of deteriorating political stability in the Congo, he felt any threat was not immediate. He also saw this as an opportunity to take a couple of weeks to travel with me to some African destinations. Of course, I was very enthusiastic.

On the 9th of January 1968, Charley drove me to Ikeja Airport for my flight to Congo Brazzaville where I was to stay overnight and continue to Kinshasa the following morning by crossing the mighty Congo River on a ferry. An awkward itinerary but full of interesting potential.

After a smooth landing in Brazzaville in early evening and changing just enough money to pay for a taxi and a ferry ticket, I headed out of the shabby airport into oppressive, equatorial heat, and took the only waiting taxi. Through drab, sad streets, the driver gave me sideways glances while muttering in a language I didn't understand. I would have enjoyed a short conversation with him about his town but was not invited to, instead I turned my head away from his gaze and watched through the open window as we descended towards the river and a very dreary-looking hotel. Evening in Brazzaville and the streets were deserted.

There was no garden, no doorman, no 'Welcome' sign, just an unadorned concrete path and steps leading to the hotel entrance. No smiles from the man checking me in. My voice echoed around the vast lobby as I used the hotel pay phone to announce my arrival to Terry who was across the river in Kinshasa, and confirm my intention to be on the first ferry the following morning. Then I took a look around. The hotel appeared to be an old bleak military barrack, stark and unadorned, all function, no frills. My room, off a narrow uncarpeted corridor, was a cubicle, about ten feet by eight feet, with a single bed and a wonky wooden chair. The high window was covered by a black canvas blind, nothing to see beyond it when I dared to stand on a corner of the hard mattress to pull it back to peek. Darkness filled the gloom outside, as well as inside, with a heavy impenetrable veil of night. Brrrr, it gave me the chills. I remember wondering if Terry had ever stayed here. A Hilton was more to his liking.

My reservation included supper, but I was the only person carrying a tray along the food line in an enormous room set up cafeteria style. Congo Brazzaville had been a French colony prior to its independence in 1960, could French culinary traditions have been maintained? I didn't think it likely. So, ignoring the possibility of enjoying something wonderfully delicious, I only nibbled on bread and cheese. I have no memory of what offerings were available as I walked past them. Once in the cafeteria, I had anticipated the food, like everything else, to be bland and boring.

An uncomfortable fitful sleep. Then avoiding the breakfast food offerings, I grabbed a coffee, which was quite tasty, and I wondered if I had been too hasty in refusing breakfast. Too late to reconsider, it was time to head down the steep rocky slope to the quay, my borrowed suitcase bumping behind me, the sun's rays already adding more warmth to the humid air. The ferry was tied up at the dock with engines humming when I bought my one-way ticket. But I needn't have bothered hurrying because this was when things started to go very wrong.

Showing the uniformed official my ticket and passport with its visas to enter Congo Brazzaville and Congo Kinshasa, I expected to be allowed to join a few passengers already waiting on the dock. Instead, he called another uniformed official over and from their conversation, I realized there was a problem. Their gestures indicated it seemed to be with my new dress. I watched in horrified surprise as my passport was flung into a desk drawer, my suitcase pushed against the far wall behind the desk. Shoving my small backpack against my chest, one of them firmly held my elbow and guided me outside into a tiny wooden hut and locked the door. I was stunned. My demands for an explanation, ignored. I was reminded of an old-fashioned outhouse, nothing to sit on, but with that recognizable smell.

What had I done to incur this surprising imprisonment?

Standing by a small, eye-level, rectangular window-like opening in the door, I watched as the first ferry of the day loaded up all manner of excited, noisy, colourfully dressed people with their livestock and baggage. I stood in my lock-up watching passengers scramble single file along the gangplank with much pushing and laughing, wishing

I could join them. Then silence, only the monstrous river coursing powerfully out to sea.

A ferry arrived from Kinshasa docking noisily with the repetition of chaotic travelers descending the gangplank and I stood and watched them filling the dock with animation and noise. And so the morning passed with increasing heat and humidity as ferry boat arrivals and departures provided me with distraction. When I had the chance to get the attention of an official looking man who actually walked close to me by intention or accident, I shouted to him to give me some information. Grateful again that I could speak French, I asked, 'What have I done?' In an accent I found difficult to understand he explained, 'In Brazzaville women do not expose their legs.' One inch above my knees, it could hardly be called a miniskirt. I told him in my best French, 'I am an international traveler with visas to enter both the Republic of Congo and Congo Brazzaville, I have friends waiting for me in Kinshasa, and if I don't arrive as planned there will be a big stink. Would you like to be a party to that?' No reply. His shiny, vacant black face turned officially from me, heading back to the office. How bold I was.

I was beginning to get a feeling for the layout of the dock in case there was an opportunity to escape. A fantastical and impossible dream. In the meantime, I decided I had to do something to remedy the length of my Lord and Taylor dress. With my Swiss Army Knife in a pocket of my backpack, I would pass the time by carefully unpicking the hem, then see how much cover that provided.

There must have been at least an inch and a half of material hidden there. Imagine the challenge I faced to unpick tiny stitches of thread, exactly the same color as the material, in the relative dark, standing up. It was laborious, tedious work. Perspiration dripped off my nose. Taking the dress off would have made the job much easier but I didn't dare do that. I seemed to have time and when my back started to complain of my bent and twisted posture, I had the luxury of standing up straight and stretching my arms above my head where there was room. Deep knee bends, balancing on one leg, standing on toes, little steps side to-side, any movement I could think of, helped in small ways. At three hundred miles south of the equator, it was airless inside the hut. The heat was crushing, so I had to muster whatever self-control I could to continue my mission. Stitch by stitch, I carefully inched my way around the hem convinced that this would contribute to my freedom. Eventually, hoping I hadn't damaged this pretty, travel dress, it was finished.

The day passed. Ferries came and went with less hustle and bustle than in the morning. The long hot afternoon with the sun right overhead slowly drew on. I was parched and beginning to feel a little woozy. With my hem project finished I wondered how many more ferries there would be before the dock closed for the night. I needed something to drink, preferably something in a bottle not a glass. As I stood at the little window, another attempt to get someone's attention paid off. I was handed a bottle of Fanta, a sugary orange drink I always avoided. Not this time. Thanking the official who had elbowed me into the hut about eight hours earlier, I repeated my concern that an international incident would develop if I wasn't allowed to take the ferry to the other side before nightfall, people were waiting for me...I had rationalized during the day that I had to be firm, strong, and cooperative with my captors, but realized they had their game plan from the beginning. I had to trust that mine: of eventually getting on the ferry, would work. And it did.

A few more hours and, tired, hot, and still thirsty, I was finally released in the dark to board: destination Kinshasa. My precious passport returned to me and safely stowed, my suitcase intact, and my skirt a little longer, though probably no-one noticed. I, alone, struggled up the long, endless gangplank, with its uneven ribs, and plopped onto the nearest hot bare metal seat. There I stayed luxuriating in relative comfort, my aching legs relieved at last. A black sky sprinkled with stars and the chug, chug of the engine turning the vessel into the muddy current, calmed my frustration. I took greedy gulps of fresh air, felt the warm wind in my hair and watched the lights of Kinshasa harbour get closer and closer. Soon I knew my ordeal would be over.

There was the familiar face and two more beside him: Terry, Pelle, Mereta were waiting for me on the dock, waving and cheering as I wobbled down the gangplank. They had been to meet every ferry from Brazzaville all day long.

Welcome at last to Congo Kinshasa!

After Thoughts

Behind the scenes, those political troubles brewing in the Republic of Congo, cut short the two weeks Terry had planned to vacation there. Instead, we stayed with Pelle and Mereta for two days and then spent two weeks visiting Johannesburg, Cape Town, Madrid, and Paris. A total of six very different countries: Nigeria, Congo Brazzaville, Republic of Congo, South Africa, Spain, and France.

I was proud of the way I had handled those travel challenges. I'd learned that Brazzaville was a country of slow-moving political change following France's departure in 1960. And Kinshasa, the bustling energetic capitol of the Congo, was still trying to find its identity in a country searching for balanced cooperation between the old tribal allegiances and the turmoil caused by independence following Belgium's departure eight years previously. I thought the difference between the two Congos was the discrepancy between their wealth. For several generations, Belgium had plundered millions of tons of precious metals from Congo Kinshasa's incredible natural resources, then President Mobutu Sese Seko, as he gained in power and control, continued a personal pillage that created an enormous population of poor, confused Congolese. I saw a continuation of deep discontent. While in Nigeria there was a cruel, inhumane civil war raging since 1967 that I knew so little about at that time.

Eventually I understood why I was put out of sight until dark of night when my short skirt was less obvious, less disrespectful to Brazzaville and its people. The rationale was part political, part tribal traditions, part male domination, and part religious, especially if Muslim guardianship rules were in place. I didn't know and Terry didn't either.

In subsequent travels up and down the continent, during casual conversations, women would share their frustration with their government's social policies. Zambia, for example, also had laws referencing women's fashion, preventing ladies from showing too much leg. I had learned the lesson by the time I went there. In the 1960s, English and European magazines carried photographs of mini-skirted African actresses and singers. Photographs that inspired young Zambian teachers, secretaries, mothers, bus conductors for example, to want that freedom also. They wanted to enjoy the consequences of earning a wage by expressing themselves in the way their international contemporaries did, by joining the Women's Liberation Movement and proudly wearing short skirts. Their struggle would continue for years.

7

Settling Into Lagos

In January 1968, I was accepted into the family of pilots living at the Federal Palace Hotel, close to the airport, a home of sorts for the team of Terry and his mercenary friends, who were flying for the Nigerian military government. His contract was to teach airmen to fly helicopters for the air force, I didn't know what responsibility the others had. They were all men of courage and adventure.

Having once again managed to leave a sinking ship at the last minute, (flying for Mobutu), Terry had exited the Congo and moved north to Nigeria where his old, pilot friends had escaped to earlier. They would be together again flying in that country's war effort, another civil war. Just his cup of tea.

On the 6th parallel, Lagos was hot and humid, dripping hot. The constant indoor/outdoor contrast took some getting used to. I had no kitchen, or garden, sewing machine, or friends. No theatre, symphony, or work, and only a freezing hotel room for privacy. Regardless of what I didn't have, I was very happy to be the only European woman at the hotel and to spend my days with a book or magazine I found, to luxuriate in the coolness of the pool. With purloined paper from the front desk, I would write copious letters to family and friends around the world. I enjoyed sipping tea as I sat in the comfortable lounge with its deep brocade covered armchairs and wide clean windows looking onto tropical greenery beyond. The hotel staff spoke English and, since the country had gained independence from Britain only eight years previously, they were familiar and comfortable with foreigners.

Being on my own during the days and spending my nights in the company of the men in the bar and dining room became my life. It was a strange existence not to have any responsibilities other than being present.

My situation improved considerably when Helen, the wife of one of the Belgian pilots arrived. I felt she legitimized my presence. My French, again, came in handy. I had daytime company. We could gossip. She entertained me with stories of her long relationship with her mercenary husband who followed fortunes and wars all over Africa. I was fascinated. She unwittingly opened a window in my awareness that allowed me to see, voyeur-like, the risks the men were taking, not for some cause they believed in, but for a contract they had signed.

I'd been learning not to ask questions or expect explanations since Terry had entered my life. There was plenty to distract me from questioning him, but I was curious. I would try different ways to get information. As an occupational therapist, a problem solver, a person with plenty of ideas, I wasn't successful. Instead my inquisitiveness annoyed Terry. He didn't like me voicing helpful advice when I could see solutions to problems. I'm sure I spoke up then and continued to over the twenty years we spent together. He would say, 'Joan always has a better idea,' as if that were a crime.

As the weeks turned to months, I became comfortably familiar with Lagos and really enjoyed living there. Everything I saw and heard fascinated me. Everything about Lagos and the hotel was strange, from the inescapable antiseptic smell of the hotel elevators and hallways to the hodgepodge of traffic and pedestrians filling the streets in crazy unpredictability. I loved the overpowering heat, the cool contrast of the sparkling pool, the audacious flowers, the constant background noises, the bustle, hum and honks of traffic, the candle lit nights when a drive anywhere was strangely mesmerizing.

In 1968, with many parts of Lagos without electric power, unpaved roads were unlit at night, and because the heat didn't significantly dissipate with sunset, people sat outside late in the evenings on wooden crates in front of their small shops. Joined by friends and family, the circles of people grew in size with noisy conversations issuing from expressive black faces. Candles provided light but many stalls used fire in a nearby brazier to add brightness. With the combination of dust stirred up by cars and miles of smokey fires lining roads, the nighttime air was as ghostly as a sandstorm and just as mysterious.

Around the communal hotel dining table, I noticed Helen always managed to steer conversations to subjects not related to work that engaged her husband and his friends. I wanted to know how far away the war actually was. Although I might never have known it was a war that had brought them all together, the references to it were subliminal even to my trained therapist's ear.

But the war did have a small influence on us as hotel residents. We were used to gathering in the dining room at each day's end to have a social drink and unwind from stresses before ordering our meals. The food offered was excellent, as was the wine, until we eventually drank the cellar dry and there were higher priorities for the hotel than restocking their wine supply. The discovery was announced, with apologies, by the *maître d'.* We understood he could do nothing. It was one of the tragedies of war and we were devastated.

We had taken the excellent wine supply for granted. Now what?

Aren't good ideas born of disaster? Noticing that the dining room walls were decorated with bunches of fake red and faded green grapes with green plastic leaves draped around wine bottles held in black wrought iron brackets, someone casually asked the *maître d'* if those wine bottles were full of wine (this was one of my best ideas): having been there for so long, no one remembered. Terry suggested he take a bottle down and check it out. Holding the bottle in its reclined position, as gently as if it were a baby, he blew off dust clouds before carefully wiping it. It felt full. We all held our breath. He cradled a bottle of 1948 Chateau Neuf du Pape. With the care it demanded, he pulled the cork, gave it a sniff, and offered a taste to Terry. 'Umm, not bad, it's drinkable.' It needed to breathe, but it was wonderful, after all, it had been stored in a relatively cool room, neck down, undisturbed for perhaps twenty years and it wasn't alone.

Clusters of bottles and their plastic greenery adorned all the walls. We told the maître d' we'd make do with them if he agreed. I don't think we fooled him for a moment, he was happy to go along with our ruse. A good man. The wines were all perfectly delicious, every one of them. Not only Chateau Neuf du Pape, but Margaux and Pommard, those I remember because I had never tasted wines quite so smooth and delicious. As the weeks passed, we drank every last bottle with gratitude to a well-trained sommelier who, proud of the cellar he was curating, had used the best wines to complement the hotel's excellent dining room ambiance. It's possible I also made the suggestion to return the empty bottles to their metal cradles amid the fake grapes and leaves so that, except for a noticeable lack of dust, the room looked as if nothing had been changed.

8

Biafra Beckons

Week-end spring skiing with my friends in the Laurentian mountains, north of *Montréal*, was excellent that year. Also satisfying was my part-time job at Maimonides Hospital, close to my father's home where I was staying during the three month sojourn Terry needed to visit people in Maine, Washington DC, and New York City. He frequently drove between those three destinations and flew to visit me a couple of times. I had no clue why the people he visited were so important and even my crafty attempts to question him were failures. We returned to Nigeria and the Federal Palace Hotel in April 1968.

Since Helen had returned to Brussels, I was the only woman again at the pilot's dining table: I was in their midst, with my ears wide open for any information I could glean from their conversations. Mealtime discussions were becoming full of concern and frustration. There was a new disturbing discomfort, a palpable undercurrent of an impending need for change. Nothing was said to me.

Every day they were off flying, where, what, or why I didn't know. I did know that all of them, except Terry, were flying fixed wing aircraft. Although he loved to teach aspiring helicopter pilots and did it really well, it wasn't enough of a challenge, nor did it satisfy his need for responsibility. Perhaps they all were feeling dissatisfied. I was aware of and respected the long-standing friendships and trust existing between Terry, Ares, Charlie, Henri, and Pierre They had supported one another in many dangerous Congo adventures. Ares had stayed with me in *Montréal* when he was between jobs. They all seemed to be living from day to day on a knife's edge of uncertainty. Eventually it was time for change.

———

By the end of April, the hotel entourage had dispersed. How would such a serious disruption affect me? Living successfully in Africa with Terry was built on my trust in him, and from his actions I believed he would consider my safety and well-being as well as his own. But with the break-up of the Federal Palace Hotel group of friends I realized how vulnerable I could be. What would I do if suddenly alone in Lagos without a home? I kept my concerns to myself safe in the knowledge that, while working for those three months at Maimonides hospital, I'd made enough money to purchase an open-ticket to fly from Lagos to *Montréal* in case I needed it.

Terry and I found a small ground-floor apartment in Ikeja, and I found part-time work at the Military Rehabilitation Hospital as an occupational therapist. The soldiers I worked with had been on the front lines of war, the war that was beginning to encroach on my life in unexpected ways. Some of the students Terry was teaching were Igbo (pronounced 'ee-bo' or 'i-bō') tribal members, smart, well-coordinated, eager to learn. A pleasure to teach. He was a masterful teacher, and although I enjoyed taking the controls in a fixed wing aircraft, I was never brave enough to handle a helicopter, even with him sitting beside me.

During that summer, Terry would invite me to join a Saturday training flight. He would be teaching with twin controls, sitting in the right-hand seat, the student in the left doing the flying. I'd ride in the back quite happily. Although flights were to towns north of Lagos deep in Biafra, I had no understanding they were towns touched by the terror of war.

Then, returning from Kaduna, his hometown in the north, a student had to fly through and around a tremendous storm with lightning slicing the sky so close to us we could hear the crackle, deafening thunder, rain pounding the cockpit. He stayed calm and in control doing a superb job, landing us safely at Lagos airport in heavy rain. Of all the students, I enjoyed flying with him the most. As we walked back to the airport hangar in the continuing deluge, he gave me a clue about the location of the war: he told me he had buried all his money and a couple of guns in his garden as insurance against the possibility of his demise. His family would know where to find them.

———

Chance meetings; job offers, promises to pay back favours, were frequent occurrences in Terry's life. Often the timing was totally unpredictable; he'd give a great sigh of relief as if to say, 'Saved again.'

One such meeting in mid-September, occurred between Terry and an American called Robert Robards, a helicopter charter entrepreneur contracted with UNICEF (*United Nations International Children's Emergency Fund*) to establish a rescue mission out of Calabar, Biafra. There were shenanigans. Although Robards had lined up a team of volunteers who had responded to his newspaper and TV commercials in America, the helicopters he had purchased in Texas were mechanically unreliable. At age thirty-five, he didn't have the experience to operate such a demanding, dangerous mission. Terry, although two years younger than Robards, saw this opportunity to impress him that he, Terry, was the man to do the job, and was on his way to New York for interviews at the United Nations in a matter of two weeks.

This was exactly the sort of humanitarian challenge Terry was hoping for. Assigned to take on the responsibility by U.N. administration, he quickly got to work using all his organizational and administrative skills powered by absolute determination that he would make the mission a success. For me, it was a silent understanding that he wouldn't be able to supervise a relief mission in Biafra from Lagos, it would mean eventually making a move to the town where the mission would be located: Calabar.

Subsequently, Robards managed to locate two heavy-duty H-34 helicopters in Tel Aviv, Israel. But in order to fly them safely around the west African coast and across the Sahara to Nigeria through many Muslim countries, Terry insisted that every trace of Israeli writing and identifying marks had to be removed.

———

While that was being done, we saw an opportunity to take a vacation to attend the Opening and first week of the 10th Olympic Games in Mexico City in mid-October.

With seats in the stadium for all the track and field events we saw the new way to do the high-jump: the Fosbury Flop, and the Human Rights salute protest by Americans Smith and Carlos which resulted in their unfortunate removal from the Games, without their gold and bronze medals. But what moved me most about the Games was what happened as the Czechoslovakian team entered the Stadium during the Opening Ceremony. Just two months earlier the Soviet Union had invaded their country in an attempt to control freedom of speech and impose other reforms. Aware of that invasion, thousands spectators from all over the world spontaneously stood up, stamped their feet, clapped their hands, shouted their support non-stop as the team slowly circled the track, proudly following their flag. It was both exhilarating and fatiguing at more than 7,000 ft elevation. That outpouring of support deeply touched me.

Being in Mexico City was a real vacation, but every day sitting to watch amazing feats of physical prowess was tiring. Although the competitions were wonderful, the stadium was hot, smelly, and crowded. How I longed for some open space, greenery and fresh air. To satisfy my cravings, Terry suggested taking an afternoon off to go horseback riding up a mountain to explore and admire the view. Perfect. Riding my *Caballo Blanco* was like floating on a cloud, his movements so smooth and gentle. But Terry's mount, *Caballo Negro* had ideas of his own. For a while, they both disappeared, sheepishly reappearing through trees half way up trail. Eventually on the mountain top we were greeted by cool, clean breezes loaded with evergreen perfume, and long far-away vistas to distant mountains across the smoldering city. Claustrophobia left me as we walked along paths through the forest, I felt calm but hardly refreshed. Now the challenge was how to quench my thirst. The only available drink up there was *pulque*, a dirty-looking, very rough, hard liquor we had to try. (One sip was enough to know it wasn't going to help). So we returned to where the horses were tethered to a tree and made a slow and easy swaying ride down the mountain path. It had been a successful afternoon. After many sips of water, my transformation was complete and I was ready to return to the Games.

⁓

With our vacation over, I managed a quick return to *Montréal* for my brother's birthday, and Terry, eager to get on with his project, flew directly to Tel Aviv. He was immediately immersed in inspecting the preparations of the two H-34's; welcoming and orienting a new volunteer crew Robards had put together and by mid-November he had most of the ferrying organization planned and the helicopters almost ready to roll. I arrived there after long, tiring flights from Canada with layovers in Paris and Athens. The men were still working on their meal when a taxi dropped me off at the restaurant with my backpack. There were four people at the round table when Terry stood to greet and introduce me. What a mixed bunch they were: Bob Billings, a United Airlines pilot ex-Marine; Joe McGinity, an executive with Chase Manhattan Bank and ex-Marine pilot; and Jerry Gauntlett an ex-R.A.F.

mechanic/engineer. I was so exhausted I remember falling asleep at that supper table with my head in my dinner. Not my best first impression.

A week later the two helicopters were ready for the long, dangerous ferry from Israel to Nigeria. Having enjoyed exploring Tel Aviv on my own, especially walking on the beach and watching the elderly Tel Avivans exercising every morning, I joined the men and their helicopters in Jerusalem and, on 21st November, set off with them for Greece, the first leg of their five thousand mile flying marathon. However, a few hours out over the sea, a fuel line problem in Billings' aircraft forced the helicopters to land in Larnaca, Cyprus. Repairs were made quickly, and we carried on to Rhodes and Athens where we stayed overnight. If we hadn't been flying low over the most historic, beautiful, ancient countries of Corfu, Albania, and the deep blue Mediterranean, I would not have managed to crouch to look out of the tiny window, hour after hour, in the cold, cavernous back of an H-34 with Billings' heavy hardhat bouncing around on my head and his great wool coat over my shoulders. At the end of each long day, I was left feeling exhilarated and exhausted. I loved every minute.

Rome, the next stop, was where the banker decided a trip to the Vatican might be better use of his time, leaving Terry, Billings, and Gauntlet, to continue in the two helicopters.

They would fly to Marseilles in southern France, make one stop in the south of Spain, and across the Mediterranean to Morocco, Africa and the official start of their epic journey to Calabar in the Southeast corner of Nigeria. On 23rd November 1968, I stood on the tarmac as the men climbed aboard. With a brave smile; crossed fingers of one hand hidden behind my back, I waved goodbye to the two huge white machines with their human cargo of three, as they took off at Rome's Fiumicino airport.

After enough excitement and dizzying travel, I took a train to Ostia, ancient Roman seaside town to visit Italian friends and their two dogs for a couple of calm and quiet weeks, walking with them along the beach, cooking up veal parmigianas, cannolis and other Italian treats. During that respite there was sparse contact from the helicopter crew while they headed towards Morocco. The next seemingly endless thousands of miles would challenge the capacity of the helicopters, and the skill and stamina of the crew to fly very long distances over hot empty deserts without any back up and no one tracking their progress. A huge achievement if they could do it.

With the passing of eight days and no word of their estimated time of arrival in Nigeria, I made no more entries in my diary for 1968.

9

Our Calabar and the Genesis of War

They safely landed at the airport in Lagos.

It was mid-January1969. Until I read Terry's biography in 2011[1], I knew nothing about the many serious adventures the three men experienced as they traversed the African deserts west to east. The men were all droopy and disheveled, absolutely exhausted, having successfully flown an incredible nearly five thousand miles from Tel Aviv in Israel completely on their own. They had flown around mountains and across vast emptiness in a feat of enormous skill, determination, and fortitude.

Calabar

The ferrying was over. But there was one more leg to fly: Lagos to Calabar, Biafra. I joined them, along with my Igbo houseman, Jacob, who was taking advantage of a ride in the back of a helicopter to escape dangers to his life if

---

1 For more about Terry Peet refer to his biography: *Renegade Hero* by Michael Hingston, published in 2011 by Pen and Sword Books Limited, London

he stayed in Lagos. We were two extra pieces of cargo not included on the manifest.

The helicopters were refueled and, within the day, we all headed to Calabar in Nigeria's Eastern State, home of the Igbo people. We arrived in early afternoon, Terry, Jacob, and I would immediately get to work. Billings and Gauntlet would soon return to their homes in California and UK respectively.

During the previous year at the hotel in Ikeja, I'd heard no details about the Biafran war even though the pilots flew over and into it daily. However, on my trip back to *Montréal* for New Year 1969, while I waited for Terry to return to Lagos with the helicopters, I'd read newspapers about the horrors and at last, understood his hesitation to include me in our dinner table conversations. I'd read and heard enough to convince me to find some useful way to help Biafra's 'David' defy the federal army's 'Goliath' once I got into the state.

And there I was.

———

I listened with interest as Terry shot out his ideas and plans for how he would take on this new challenge, he saw managing the UNICEF Relief Mission as an opportunity to put all his skills to use. He'd proven his ability to fly and expedite a long, complicated flight plan. Now he ruminated on how he would test his ability to organize a team of pilots and ground crew he hadn't yet met, men who would work long hours under grueling conditions with very few comforts. But I had no idea what being in Calabar would mean for me. Were there expectations I hadn't been told about? I quietly decided to make the most of every day. If there was an opportunity to contribute to or support the mission, I would happily step up to the challenge.

The Genesis of War

Calabar was located five miles inland from the Cross River estuary that opened to the Gulf of Guinea in that 90° corner on Africa's west coast. Having a deep harbour with access to ocean-going ships was strategically valuable to Biafra; it was the reason why the town was targeted early on for destruction once war was declared in July 1967. It was also why Calabar was chosen by UNICEF as a base of operations for its Relief Mission.

Built on the banks of the river and nestled around the base of the small hill, Calabar had a famous, well-preserved, historic district going back to the days of slavery. Before the war, it had been a bustling community with many successful industries, in particular a German owned cement factory that had provided building materials for the growing town and its smaller neighbours. The two-story school, of which the local people were extremely proud, was made of concrete.

———

Historically, hatred expressed by the federal government against the Igbo people and their nearby tribal cousins had been slowly gathering momentum since Britain had pulled out of Nigeria as a colonial presence in 1960. Hatred exploded in the summer of 1966 with brutal mass slaughter of Igbo people starting in the Muslim north and spreading through northern and central Nigeria. Hatred moved like a slow mud slide through town after town. Those who were able, fled to the Eastern State of Biafra, the Igbo homeland. It was a time of terrible bloodshed with knives and machetes. Young and old men, women, and children were beheaded, disemboweled, massacred and mutilated, and the killing spree followed the fleeing Igbos across the country.

Although I had read newspapers during my stay in Canada, I knew so few details about what was happening until I read chilling firsthand reports in Frederick Forsyth's book *The Biafra Story*[2]. His explanations helped

---

2 *The Biafra Story, The Making of an African Legend* by: Frederick Forsyth, 2001, published by: Pen and Sword Books Ltd., London

me understand the Igbo people's point of view and their deep cultural values, which, as I became familiar with Jacob, my house-man, and as I lived among the Igbo people in Calabar, I saw truth in his interpretations.

What could possibly have driven the Emirs of northern towns like Kano to encourage such a frenzy of killing? Forsyth, who was in Biafra reporting for the BBC, describes how he learned that the very nature of Igbo people was their downfall. Their strong Christian ethic, dedication and diligence motivated thousands of men and their families to spread across the country into many communities for employment. Their decency, reliability and precious education allowed them to step into all sorts of jobs and get the work done. Without intending to, they made themselves indispensable and hated. For example, when Igbos fled *en mass* from the capital, Lagos, government offices ceased to operate; there was no one remaining who knew how to administer the business of government.

———

It was an Igbo genocide and the first terrifying blow to Colonel Ojukwu's dream of independence for his Biafran state. He was the much loved and respected leader of the Igbo people.

Forsyth's reports followed seriously deteriorating circumstances for Biafra. As in the late spring of 1967, when Colonel Yakabu Gowan, the Nigerian Military leader, imposed a comprehensive blockade on the state that included commercial flights to and from Lagos, post office and telephone services, food supplies, and more. These brought economic and social isolation that were interpreted as a second costly blow to independence.

But when vast amounts of extremely high-quality oil were discovered under the Biafran soil near Port Harcourt, the greedy federal government saw it as belonging to them. Col. Gowan believed he had to have it for the wealth and empowerment it would provide his government. A third blow to the Biafran goal of independence.

At this, Col. Ojukwu said, 'Enough.'

With the support of his state and local governments, Colonel Ojukwu decided to secede from Nigeria. The decision was by no means rushed, the possibility had been foreseen. But by then in early summer, secession was necessary. A withdrawal from the country of Nigeria would both secure oil revenues for Biafra and maintain the state's autonomy.

It turned out to be a very brave and dangerous decision, but the story wasn't over.

Abandonment by Biafra so provoked Col. Gowan, who had promised to maintain a united Nigeria as part of his presidential platform, that he declared war on Biafra in July 1967.

At this point the Biafran government realized the need to sabotage Calabar's port to prevent federal ships from advancing inland with all their weapons, munitions and personnel of war. It was a successful ploy which probably did protect the town and points further north for a few months, at least until October. That's when the federal Army's Colonel Adekunle launched his military assault named *Operation Tiger Claw*[3]: a flotilla of armed ships that approached Calabar from the south, each filled with well-trained commando troops. He and his soldiers, with their British and Soviet supplied weaponry, stormed through Calabar on foot for two days, demolishing everything. Leaving it ransacked and in ruin, clouds of dust filled the air. Biafran forces had put up a brave resistance but were unable to successfully rebuff the larger, stronger enemy.

Calabar was in ruins, but its people were not defeated. They rallied to plan and create ways to protect and support the town and their people to the north since Adekunle's army was heading in that direction when he left Calabar.

3 Wikipedia. Operation Tiger Claw. Two Wikipedia sources I consulted provided different stories I have pieced together. Lasting two days, the battle was chaotic, and poorly reported.

First, the port was restored to its previous function so that friendly ships could bring in essential relief supplies. By the sheer force of their ingenuity, they succeeded in revitalizing necessary infrastructure.

When we arrived in January 1969, trying to imagine how the town had been fifteen months earlier was difficult. I couldn't believe the destruction had been so complete. Because quickly roofs, windows, walls, electricity and water supplies were repaired. The hospital was also restored (as demanded by Col. Adekunle for the care and recovery of his traumatized soldiers). True, the cement factory was destroyed and gone, but a refugee camp was created in a derelict concrete workshop and the school had only been abandoned. All the pot-holed roads told the story.

To people in countries around the world, Biafra's plight touched an emotional nerve, as was intended by Col. Ojukwu with his photographs of starving children. Perhaps that was what encouraged two new pilots, a loadmaster, and a mechanic, to respond to Mr. Robard's second round of advertising on American television that capitalized on the hardships of children. The helicopter relief mission was Robards' idea. He had convinced the United Nations and the federal government [4] to provide the funding he would

---

4 I knew there was federal money contributing to the mission but was unable to find a reference to explain how that happened.

need to move tonnes of donated food from the harbour north to war zones where starvation was a weapon chosen by Colonel Gowan. As it turned out, his motivation might not have been wholly altruistic.

More About Calabar

A crew arrived to work in late 1968 while the two helicopters were being ferried around the vast bulge of Africa, and once the new pilots had taken possession of the forlorn school, they had started to fly relief flights from the harbour to northern war zones doing their best without any supervision. Once word got out to the townsfolk that the 'pilots' had established themselves in the old school, the building's name morphed into the 'Palace', and stuck! Using the school as their headquarters and classrooms as makeshift apartments turned out to be a brilliant idea for Terry's operation because the large, not-very-grassy playground became a perfect location for helicopter landings, take offs, refueling, maintenance and parking. There was enough indoor space to accommodate a crew of local men to cook, wash and clean for them, all Igbo tribal members with that strong work ethic and good education. Their names were Wednesday, Friday and Sunday, and when our Jacob arrived, he made the Palace his home too.

These new helicopter recruits, all American beefy ex-military men, had been working and doing a decent job, but hadn't been paid for a month by Mr. Robards who was in New York. Initially, they were not impressed with their new boss, a Brit. But Terry gained their support and cooperation by promising them a consistent supply of cold beer and a regular pay cheque. The UNICEF Relief Mission team was created.

As well as taking on the responsibility of starting food distribution flights, someone in that crew must have negotiated with the town to find a home for the rest of the team, Terry, Jacob, and me. Because on the day we arrived in Calabar, Jacob was swept away to the Palace and Terry and I were marched to an abandoned German cement-factory employee's house on the pot-holed road leading up the small hill above the school, where I started to make a home for us. The town obviously had been evacuated in such a hurry, we were able to use all the previous occupants' possessions in the kitchen, living room, and three bedrooms. We simply took over what was there.

Terry got to work immediately. There was no time for rest and relaxation even though he had just completed that monumental flying marathon. Exhaustion was replaced by adrenaline. He had delivered the two H-34 helicopters. He had a qualified crew. The mission's success was going to be entirely up to him. A daunting responsibility, and the humanitarian challenge he'd been awaiting for years. He was invigorated.

———

Not really part of the team, did I have a role to play? Before leaving Lagos, and as I learned more about the war, I had made a personal commitment to assist the Biafran people in any way I could. I knew I'd have to entertain and charm visiting dignitaries occasionally and keep a comfortable home for the hero to return to at the end of each long, hot day. Was that it?

No. I would be open to opportunities beyond my imagination and, as Mary Oliver said, 'Instructions for living: Pay attention. Be astonished. Tell about it.' I would do that.

10

The Power of Touch

Too often we underestimate the power of a touch,
a smile, a kind word, a listening ear, an honest
compliment, or the smallest act of caring, all of which
have the potential to turn a life around.

~ Leo Buscaglia

Where was this war?

We were finally established in Calabar, Eastern Province
of Nigeria. Four helicopters were parked on the school
playground: the two H-34s, one large H-19, and a small
Fairchild Hiller. The crew consisted of two pilots, one
engineer, a load master and Terry, who, doubling as a pilot,
was in charge of this United Nations project. Their mission
for being in Calabar, was to break the food blockade
imposed by the federal government to essentially starve the
Biafran people into abandoning their goal of independence
from Nigeria. We all were very busy. With the war off in
the distance I still didn't have a clear idea of where we were
in relation to that big picture.

In early 1969, I watched the pilots climb into their helicopters, buckle in, give the 'all clear' and take off with tonnes of food they had picked up from the harbour. How many times a day did they travel back and forth, over and over, without any down time except when the machine was being refueled? That's when they could grab some lunch and water and a little walk for exercise. It was the same grueling schedule they had maintained since before Terry arrived and continued to after. And that's why his promise of cold beer and a paycheck was so important. I saw their dedication.

Without a newspaper or radio to fill me in, I was living in a state of ignorance. Did it matter that I had no idea where the action actually was? I had been to towns in the north of Biafra with student helicopter pilots when we were living in Lagos, paying very little attention to how far we flew in miles or time, and without seeing any obvious evidence of war in the towns we visited. It was enough for me to know the war was real, and somewhere off to the north.

It wasn't until I ventured away from the Palace and home that I confronted reality.

Within a day of my arrival I discovered our neighbours up the hill, an English lady called Margaret Clark; her husband Ron, was the Harbour Master for the Calabar docks. They and their two young children, Allison and Sean, had been living there for more than a year. We became immediate friends. When I shared with Margaret that I was wondering what I could do to help the townsfolk, she told me about a refugee camp just a mile away from the Palace. She had been an occasional visitor and suggested I might find it interesting, so I took her advice and volunteered without knowing what to expect.

This facility was housed in a single-story concrete building which, before the war, could have served any purpose; a factory, warehouse, offices. There was a large walled open space in front, perhaps originally a simple garden, now empty of clues; just corrugated, bare earth, its wall in need of serious repair. It might have been a private, successful Igbo business that was quickly abandoned. Or possibly it was some old foreigner's commercial undertaking before the military rampage quickly scattered all European expatriates back to their homes in far-away countries in October 1967.

The building looked beaten. It was blackened outside and dark inside. It smelt damp. I interpreted the bare, low-wattage bulbs hanging from the ceiling to be an attempt to create some semblance of hospitality. Nothing could soften the wooden chairs scattered about so a child could curl up in one and feel safe. This camp, a hub of refugee services, was one of two operated by the International Red Cross, its main purpose was to register newly arrived refugees and assess their needs: medical, accommodation, nutritional. Where was the questioning taking place and who was asking the questions? Were any services provided there, was a doctor on site? I only saw the crowd of numb people as they swept into the reception area.

Terry Crawley was the English man responsible for the Red Cross missions and was soon to be a friend of ours. He probably had an office there, but we never met at the facility. Terry and I started to invite him to our home and I knew from his evening visits that he was constantly on the move negotiating with the Minister of Rehabilitation for support; with government and international officials for food, medical supplies, and housing and with my Terry for UNICEF's helicopter food deliveries.

Arriving at the camp in the mornings on my deux chevaux (a two horse-power bike I somehow inherited) and seeing that bodies had been rolled over huge bags of donated dried food to rest against the perimeter wall for removal was a shocking way to start the day. They had died in the night, dressed only in their rags, shoe-less, flies everywhere.

But when the monsoon rains came to make a mud bath of the enclosure's bare earth, those food bags became useful as steppingstones across the slippery ground. It rained so hard, sodden paper bags of powdered milk would split open, and the escaped powder, carried down the slope by determined rivulets, made zebra skin designs across the yard, a sort of macabre *art nouveau*. I never got used to seeing the dead bodies lying against the wall or the bags of donated food used intentionally as stepping-stones. Considering there was no milk in the Igbo diet, what harm to use those donations in a more practical way?

On my visits, I only got as far as the reception area where an enormous number of forlorn, starving refugees congregated, some adults, but mostly bewildered children with expressionless faces who walked aimlessly along the walls, rocked as they sat on the hard concrete floor, staring out of the large window.

If these children were old enough to have attended school, they would speak and understand English as well as their tribal language, but there were no conversations I could share, no animated interactions, these were severely traumatized youngsters.

How could I be useful there? Ignored by all, I initially rationalized that I was the wrong colour and wondered if it was possible that children from up country had never seen a white face. Did my presence shout 'enemy' to them? Did

I add to their fear and discomfort? No. I worked hard not to. I stopped trying to analyze the situation and accepted that all the refugees, young and old, had experienced the most terrible trauma and, for the first time in my life, I was face to face with its devastating effects. On my subsequent visits my solution was to assume the identity of a quiet, practically invisible, undemanding presence, with a partial smile.

I avoided direct eye contact which could be a threat, but what could I do to break through their apathy, how could I support them? It was long before the days of Sensory Integration. The occupational therapist in me was frustrated. Until one day as I sat on the floor humming near a child lost in far-away thoughts, I had some success when I gently, slowly leaned in, the young girl didn't back away as we touched and I was able to stay shoulder to shoulder for several seconds, no more. Her taut body softened a little. I was being introduced to the power of human touch, a gift, and the best I could do, which I did, over and over and over during following days and weeks. What a lesson for me.

After a few hours, and with an achy heart, I'd grab my bike for a slow ride home along the damaged roads, letting the potholes absorb my fatigue.

Soon I'd be home with Jacob and a cup of tea, Allison, Sean and Margaret would burst in with a story to tell, followed by Ron and eventually Terry, and perhaps Terry Crawley. The evenings brought comfort and some relief. I knew we were all doing our best, but as the weeks passed it became harder and harder for me to face the terrible torment of so much suffering, even with the meditative presence of Rouen's rose window in my memory.

11

George the Cow

After about three weeks living in Calabar, we were settled into familiar routines with our friendly English family next door, the Red Cross contingent, and the helicopter team at the Palace. Pilots would fly from sunrise to sunset. It was a hot, demanding work routine. As manager of the helicopter mission, Terry had negotiated to co-ordinate services with his friend Terry Crawley of the Red Cross, an important improvement to avoid duplication of services. For money to cover many immediate needs like spare parts, fuel, food, beer, wages and unknown future expenditures, Terry frequently would have to plead in person with Mr. Robards, at his recently established base in a Lagos hotel. But the new, closer proximity between Robards and his crew, hadn't improved the continuous, frustrating, financial situation.

I would start my day with Jacob, finding out what he needed to keep our home and the helicopter team's Palace equipped not only with food but cleaning and laundry necessities. I'd advise him of any expected overnight visitors or friends invited for a meal. Then I'd jump on my deux chevaux and head over to the refugee camp to volunteer and save my errands for the afternoon. The town wasn't large but in the heat and dust, the bike was an efficient and comfortable way to get around. Sometimes I'd plan to have a cup of tea with Margaret and play with her children. With the no more than twenty Europeans in Calabar at any time we would often socialize in the evenings. The unexpected was always a possibility I had to quickly factor into these routines.

One late afternoon as the helicopters had flown in to refuel, our routine was interrupted by the arrival of a tired old Fulani cattle herder who brought his cows to graze on what little grass there was in the school playground. It would be a short, overnight respite for him. His cows were on their way to the stockyard near the docks after a very long walk from northern Nigeria. Being Fulani was probably an asset since many of the federal troops fighting Biafrans were also from that northern province. I wondered if that was how he had managed to travel safely through places where war was rampant? How had he and his beasts crossed rivers, found food?

They were all, including him, very lean and bony, except one noticeably fat black creature who soon delivered a small black and white calf which the herder asked us to keep. His cattle were on their way to be slaughtered, after which he'd be returning to the north. The mother licked and nuzzled her little baby, it stood up on wobbly legs, she might have tried to feed it. A playing field full of cows put an early end to the flying, so we wandered up the hill to home and the Palace crew got on with their evening. We all were thinking about the calf.

In the morning the herder pleaded with us, making sure we understood that he did not want the burden of a calf on his long walk home and it wouldn't bring him any money to have it slaughtered. He probably laughed at his luck after we paid him his asking price. Everyone had agreed, we couldn't say 'no.'

Some wise person told me the calf was a 'he' and I immediately called it George. Growing up in England as I did and spending many happy years walking in the countryside, I would read signs on farmer's gates: 'BEWARE OF THE BULL.' Since George had promptly attached himself to me, I couldn't imagine that I was to mother a bull. I'd been effectively brain washed by my early experiences. So to calm that haunting memory, I continued to refer to him as a cow. That's how he became 'George the Cow.'

A newborn calf. We all rallied to look after this fragile life. Sunday and Friday cleverly built a small corral with empty fifty-gallon oil drums, but I can't report that George was impressed. He did, however, love the mush we concocted with powdered milk. When I stuck my hand deep into a bowl of milk, he would latch onto two of my fingers with a leathery tongue and a tremendous suck. From an early age he would 'head butt' me quite firmly when he wanted food, a behaviour I've since seen domestic calves in England do to their mother's udders, probably a bovine way to stimulate milk flow as human babies have an innate knack of doing. Not head butting their mother but nestling her breast.

I had no knowledge of cows. There were no reference books, no one on the end of a phone I could ask, no computers, no library. Cattle didn't thrive in the Biafran heat and there were no grassy fields on which they could spend their days idly grazing. We had no idea how to tell if indeed he was a he, it seemed that no-one else had much or any experience or interest in bovine husbandry either. I had lived with dogs all my life and knew that animals needed attention, kindness, physical touch, and play, as well as food, so I did what I could to entertain and nurture George. I would stroke his neck and tickle his ears, talk to him adoringly and occasionally give him a handful of dry porridge oats, which he loved.

In spite of our ignorance, George thrived and grew quickly in both personality and size. Soon there were small bumps on his head where I imagined horns would protrude. With increased height and strength, he learned how to escape his corral by kicking over the oil barrels. He knew where the food was, and he knew to stay within the confines of the old school playground. He took to sleeping in the shade of the parked Fairchild Hiller helicopter fuselage and, with perfect timing, would take advantage of the open front door to rush into the Palace's living room. There he would ignore all attempts at distraction by planting his legs rigidly onto the tiles. He couldn't be budged as he peed and peed and peed, the pool growing in diameter, and all of us watching in amused helplessness, several mops at the ready.

He loved to trot behind me as I rode my deux chevaux around Calabar to do my errands. I remember once taking a sloping left turn a bit too quickly on an unpaved, gravely track that led down to a tiny shop where I'd buy canned sardines and salted crackers. Suddenly off balance, the bike skidded, and I slid painfully sideways onto the dirt. George disappeared; this had never happened before. Locals, there were always onlookers, enjoying my antics with George, tried to hide their giggles by covering their mouths, as the contents of my shopping bags scattered over the rough, dry path. The skid outlined by a trail of dried beans. While I gathered my skirt around my bare legs, I called George. Then feeling wretchedly embarrassed, collected what I could of my shopping. I knew their laughter wasn't cruel, they were amused.

George the Cow

George always came with me to the temporary market on a track down to the river, about a mile from the Palace. This once-a-week market, selling meat on a square of bare dirt, was an open-air event with attempts at awnings to protect against sun or rain. Scores of flies flew freely and frantically onto all produce displayed in baskets or hanging high on hooks from a wooden frame. A wall of huge black vultures marked the periphery, their wings slightly open for ventilation as they carefully pulled animal guts through their massive beaks to catch every drop of leftover blood and debris. I would keep George close beside me as I contemplated the possibility that he could be strung from a pole, belly ripped open, his ribs sold by the pound, or his legs quartered for the soup pot.

We would wander through narrow passageways made by piles of canned fruit, cassava, those hanging animal carcasses, looking for antelope. It was the only meat I trusted. I knew from George's mother's experience that cows herded together from the north were so exhausted, thin, dehydrated, and possibly sick by the time they reached Calabar's market, their meat would not be fit or safe to eat. I don't recall anyone I fed ever being ill from the antelope I prepared. That was a serious consideration, as I often had the responsibility of feeding UNICEF officials who would arrive, sometimes unannounced, expecting us to host them.

Without intending to, we had created a therapeutic family-like environment at the Palace and up the hill. Fortunate to have the company of George, and Ron and Margaret's two children who were still young and willing to be to be silly and playful, they gave us adults permission to be lighthearted, to have fun if we wanted or needed it. Even the pilots had to chuckle when George took his stance in the living room. I became very fond of him even if he was destined to become a bull.

12

Saved by a Mango

As a British voter, I was politically aligned with the United Kingdom's Labour party. How delighted I was to be invited to join the helicopter crew in one of the H-34 machines the day before Prime Minister, Mr. Harold Wilson, was expected to arrive in Port Harcourt for discussions with Colonel Adekunle. An order had come from the British High Commission in Lagos that a Royal Air Force (RAF) helicopter pilot flying in Calabar was needed for a special high-security flight in Port Harcourt, that pilot had to be Terry.

A couple of years earlier, Port Harcourt, southern Biafra's largest town, had been heavily targeted by Nigerian Air Force attacks and vicious ground troops, under the command of Colonel Adekunle whose nickname 'The Black Scorpion' described his reputation, his authority. He had moved on to supervise the destruction of Calabar and towns to the immediate north, then returned to Port Harcourt as the Eastern State's military commander. I wasn't aware of Adekunle's reputation. Was Terry?

Since vast deposits of crude oil had recently been discovered close to Port Harcourt the governments of Britain and Nigeria were both keenly interested. With such a large harbour and its close proximity to the open ocean, the town suddenly took on a major role of loading oil onto carrier ships for export.

———

Tensions were high when we flew into Port Harcourt's airport. Upon landing, Terry immediately went to find the Colonel to receive his instructions for the following day. The two other crew members quickly took off to refuel and locate a safe overnight holding place for the helicopter at the airport.

Alone in a strange town, I made my way on foot to the hotel. A comfortable looking, bullet pocked, old colonial style building of once-white concrete and brick that had managed to preserve some semblance of normalcy, in spite of having been strafed and bombed. While waiting alone in the hotel lounge with a glass of beer, I befriended some young Czechoslovakian doctors, all members of a medical team that would evolve in 1971 to be *'Médecins Sans Frontières'* (Doctors without Borders). They were going to have a party that evening, and we were all invited. I didn't hesitate to accept.

The room was crowded, noisy, smoky, and filled with friendly people who were letting off steam after a grueling day, a grueling week. We wandered in, found a beer, and over the din of the crowd, introduced ourselves to one of the medics as the UNICEF Helicopter Relief Mission crew from Calabar. But conversations were challenging with all the exuberant hilarity. There were four of us and about thirty of them, an international mix of tired, happy faces. Their whole team was there, not only doctors but lab techs, nurses, ground crew, administrators, ambulance drivers, without any obvious rank or seniority. So we joined them sitting on the floor as they shouted out their stories mostly in English, played guitars, drank beers and sang the song 'Hey Jude' over and over long into the early morning hours. What a party! All the stress we'd been holding onto dropped away into the secure ambiance of those welcoming people who didn't know us, though we all felt accepted. It was the first fun we'd had in months. Memories filled my head of college parties at McGill, when playing guitars, singing and drinking beer while sitting on the floor had been *de rigueur*.

Then morning came. I woke with too big a hangover after too little sleep. It was time to take the helicopter to the airport 'Arrivals' gate in preparation to meet Mr. Wilson. My head was pounding, my mouth dry, my senses all on edge. I moved carefully.

The atmosphere inside the small airport terminal building was already sweltering when Terry and I, feeling rotten, joined the excited crowd waiting for Mr. Wilson's DC-3 to land. I busied myself with my light meter in preparation to take photographs of my hero, my camera nonchalantly slung around my neck. Then, as the Prime Minister's plane touched down, Colonel Adekunle suddenly appeared by my side, dramatically grabbed my camera and wrenched the strap over my head. He was fuming.

'Don't you know this is absolutely forbidden?' he snarled, his breath hot on my face, his Black Scorpion personality suddenly obvious. He viciously opened the back of the camera and ripped out the film. I stood in shocked amazement as the shiny brown strip snaked its way to the floor. My precious photos, gone. 'I could have you shot, you know.'

Terry stepped closer. 'Yes,' he said. 'But you won't, not in front of the world's press with the British Prime Minister about to walk in, and not if you want me to fly the helicopter for you,' was his challenging remark. Adekunle laughed. 'Well, you'd better go and do it,' he grinned. 'Whew, well done Terry.'

We made a quick escape outside in the heat, Terry seemed calm, I quite stunned. Mr. Wilson's arrival presented a unique opportunity for Terry to have a few minutes of the Prime Minister's time before the official schedule got underway. I recall round-faced Mr. Wilson, not much taller than me, saying to Terry in his familiar Yorkshire accent, 'How can I help you?' and, because the Nigerian government was part sponsor of the UN mission, Terry asking him for more air support, another helicopter, more spare parts and the authority to fly a seriously ill child from Calabar to a hospital in Lagos. Under the UN contract he was forbidden to fly non refugees, which this child was, so permission had been denied and Terry's humanitarian sensibilities were frustrated. Once back in Calabar, Terry flew her anyway.

Mr. Wilson, I discovered, was supporting the cruel Nigerian government, he had no intention of ever influencing President Gowan to provide more assistance to Terry's UN mission. I was horrified when I recently made that discovery in Frederick Forsyth's: *The Biafra Story*. Mr. Wilson was after the oil. He was all for protecting Shell, the company taking the crude from Biafra for England's consumption and allowing the Nigerian government to starve to death nearly two million Biafran people in so doing. His presence in Biafra was a wicked sham. I will never forgive him.

I knew none of that as, with trembling fingers, I fastened the belt on the helicopter's right-hand seat, my head close to the noisy, frantic rotor shaft. I could not shake the miserable ache and everything that went along with being hung over, especially the dry mouth. How I longed for water, but there was none. Terry's mission was to fly the helicopter over the Prime Minister's motorcade as it progressed to the sports stadium. The limousine left the airport and we took off. Without the cockpit door in place, I could look down at the road lined with people, all shouting a welcome to the visitor. Unexpectedly, I saw their happy faces. They were all looking up at the helicopter to see me looking down at them as the Prime Minister's vehicle passed right in front of them along the road. I was the star! Realizing I had to respond or let Mr. Wilson down, I carefully leaned out and bravely gave the royal wave and a big smile all the way to the football stadium where he was to deliver his speech.

———

Once the helicopter had been parked in an empty airport lot and I was left alone, the quiet was bliss. But how and where to find water? I was beginning to feel ill, weak and drowsy. There was nothing useful or interesting in the vast hot tarmacked space, only a perimeter of wrecked buildings that had once been hangars, warehouses or offices, now derelict empty shells.

Then, a miracle. Walking slowly with an easy swaying gait, came a man with a large flat tray of fruit balanced on his head. I had to blink several times. He wasn't an apparition. His white shirt was open at the neck, loose around his waist, the long sleeves and well-worn pant legs rolled up, he walked in dusty black sandals that flopped with each step. I felt I knew this man, although that was impossible. He was local Igbo, calm under his huge hat of fruit with an unforgettable smile.

He headed directly towards the helicopter as if compelled by some unknown force. Did he know my need? Still smiling at me, he carefully unloaded the tray to put it on the ground and offered me a large yellowy-ripe mango. He didn't seem to mind when I gestured that I had no money but stood and watched me desperately tear greedily into the fruit, devouring his gift, letting the juice dribble down my chin and over my fingers. We laughed together at my enormous delight.

I was beginning to feel better when we sat down on the helicopter's skid in shade from the hulking fuselage to chat about Mr. Wilson's visit, his arrival at the football stadium, and the speech, which would soon be over. My rescuer took that as a reminder of his mission, to sell his mangoes to the thirsty crowd. When he turned and waved as he meandered across the empty lot with his basket perfectly balanced on his head, we both were smiling.

———

So many years later I wonder why the crowd lining the route Mr. Wilson's car took to the stadium showed such a warm and demonstrative welcome to the man whose colonial government had been ousted to make room for independence nine years earlier? Independence! There had been so many promises by Nigerian politicians about how they intended to govern their people fairly, peacefully, with shared insights and understanding. However, in 1969, the reality was that despite independence, Nigeria was no better off. Instead of the promised peace and wealth for all, it had been steadily sliding into the war-torn, poor, overpopulated, disorganized, militarily governed country where corruption was king. Perhaps this crowd of Nigerians was secretly hoping the British would return. I didn't know.

And how was it that when I so desperately needed a drink in the middle of an empty sun-drenched parking lot with no idea of which direction to walk to find relief, a lone man came to me with my salvation? I felt we were sharing something 'greater than' ourselves; something more than luck; more than I understood. His smile told me that he, too, was aware of something connecting us through thought or energy; through a common humanity that touches the deepest corner of our hearts and allows us to reach out to one another. Such a possibility is like a shadow, unidentified, hardly acknowledged but recognized when we open our awareness and feel it.

13

Sparky's Escape

 Soon another homeless creature made an appearance at our house on the hill. In the strange African time that was my 28th birthday, Terry gave me an Amazon Green parrot with a bright red head. How normal, yet how bizarre. I loved it immediately, decided he was male and gave him a neutral name, 'Sparky.' What a comic lover he turned out to be, a kindred spirit of sorts, even though he and George never met, they both switched on a love button within most of the members of our small ex-pat community and in some local neighbours too.

With rather high day-to-day stress levels for all of us in Calabar, being with Sparky was therapeutic. He beguiled everyone: all the UN and Red Cross visitors, all the pilots, the house men and their friends, our English neighbours, we all fell under the spell of his funny, entertaining antics and conversations. He took a liking to beer and would perch on the thick rim of Terry's tankard. Slurp-slurp-

slurp, burp! He loved snuggling onto my chest, just under my chin, inviting me to gently scratch his scrawny grey neck skin. Like J. Edgar Swoop, the eagle that wasn't very regal, in the Mason Williams' poem: 'under all those feathers he was absolutely naked.'

I don't know where Terry found him, but like so many of us, he was taken out of his natural environment. His wings were clipped. He had to live in a cage where he enjoyed being talked to, whistled at by everyone he met, and if the cage was by the open window, as it usually was, local children and friends would walk up the hill to visit him and have a chat: 'ello Sparky, wanna cracker?' When there was no-one for him to talk to, he'd walk along the window seat in the living room to watch birds outside or see his reflection and chatter, sing or whistle contentedly, or so it seemed.

Sparky could imitate sounds so well that when the finger of the law was pointed at that scoundrel Robards, the parrot was subpoenaed to give evidence of conversations he might have overheard in our home. He was flown to the lawyer's office in Lagos in a DC-3 and repeated, 'ow ya doin' mate?' 'Ready for a cuppa?' and 'Cheerio.' We could have told the prosecutor that he would be an absolutely useless witness.

He must have been exposed to his strange English accent long before coming to live with us, but imitating Sean and Allison, who were his most devoted admirers certainly enlarged his repertoire. There were few distractions in Calabar for young children who were welcome in our home. After Jacob let them in they would hurry to the cage, its door closed, and between giggles they would say something over and over to Sparky, perhaps something they'd heard their parents say in their London accented voices and eventually he'd say it back to them, it could take days. The shrieks of delight emanating from both children and bird could be so loud we'd have to cover our ears. It was impossible not to join the subsequent laughter. What power it gave the youngsters to teach a bird to talk.

It was Sparky's greatest delight to take advantage of an open living room window and, like a naughty child, jump down two feet to the ground. Since he couldn't fly, he'd go for a walk. Jacob would trot along beside the bird when he noticed the escape, eventually picking him up and bringing him home on his shoulder. Sometimes Sparky got to ride on the handlebars of Jacob's bicycle, and from the proud tilt of his head you could tell he loved to feel the wind under his wings, almost like flying.

One afternoon, when Jacob noticed Sparky's escape, the bird nonchalantly crossed the weedy strip, his small red head wobbling as he strutted down the rutted, potholed road as usual. This time he veered to the left, toward the shaded monsoon gutter. Friends who happened to be at the bottom of the hill looking up, spotted Jacob and shouted 'hello' but Jacob, looking down at them, noticed movement in the ditch. O.M.G. a snake. 'Hey, Mamba' he shouted, frantically waving to the folk who had just started to walk towards our house. I was inside when I heard him call, 'Madam, come quick' Jacob had noticed a snake, a green mamba (Dendroapsis *viridis*), slithering silently, slowly up the deep muddy trench.

I was busy making an improvised apple crumble with canned apples, nuts and cookie crumbs when I heard Jacob's urgent shout, and, as I ran to the front door, he appeared ready to hand the bird to me. With Sparky safely in his cage, I hurried outside to watch what was developing. Western green mambas use vision and speed for protection, the fact that this one was taking its time plowing through mud instead of swinging from tree branches put it at a significant disadvantage. A bite from this snake would quickly paralyze the victim's respiratory system with its neurotoxic venom. Death would be quick. No surprise then that the mamba was so feared. From a safe distance the small group of friends continued to amble up the road. There were no drums beating out the message of the snake's appearance, but somehow the African communication system spread the news. A crowd was gathering.

I knew nothing of African snakes, had never heard of any kind of mamba, green or black. Nor, during the six-seven weeks I'd been in Calabar had I ever been warned about any dangerous snakes. This was one of the most beautiful and venomous snakes on the continent, long and lean though large in girth compared to other snakes I'd seen in zoos. Its skin beautifully patterned, fractal-like, its colour an iridescent, bright leafy green (similar to Sparky's), was easily noticed as it curved and straightened in ponderous slowness making its way up the hill. Someone had suddenly materialized with a spade. Did it have to die?

Mambas are known to move very quickly, so we were lucky this snake was sauntering. Perhaps it was old, sick, sleepy or distracted by all the noise, the loud discussions about who would do the deed and when. It just continued a steady approach towards our home with its still open ground floor windows. Although I stood in frozen fascination with arms folded snugly across my pounding heart, I was caught up in the excitement. I watched from the edge of the crowd, willingly letting these Biafran neighbours take care of the situation, assuring myself they knew what to do.

Eventually, someone decided to act. I watched as the man with the spade approached the ditch, the shiny blade held high in readiness. In a flash he struck a vicious blow and then another to the snake's head, or where its neck would be, slicing over and over. The snake, a writhing, quickly moving monster whose behaviour was so unpredictably powerful, a dramatic acrobatic combination of curls and twists. With each stroke a cheer rose from the crowd. I had a horrible thought that had more spades been available, the killing might have developed into sport with all the men waging war on this once beautiful, but deadly creature. That was just my imagination. This vicarious experience seemed enough to satisfy the onlookers.

Then a surreptitious change in the crowd's disposition: a ripple of aggression emanated among them. Brought on by the need to kill? These were calm, moderate, local Igbo men. Yes, their town had been defeated and destroyed by the federal army, there had been deaths, their lives shattered. Enormous anger, hatred and sadness must have deeply affected them; yet here they were cheering on the killing of a feared wild creature. I saw it as a metaphor for retaliation against all the pain they had and were continuing to suffer. They took steps back, separating themselves from the action; some were holding onto each other.

It seemed a long, drawn-out event, as if it had happened in slow motion, but it was finally over. The decapitated snake's body, all bloody, slimy, and battered, was removed, balanced precariously over the blade of the spade that had killed it. To someone's cooking pot, I wondered? It took a while for the excitement to subside, for the crowd to disperse into groups of two or three, their conversations animated. Off they went down the hill, home, to tell their families what had happened. Jacob and I trudged up the hill, exhilarated, sad, happy, full of the story we told over and over to each other and to all our visitors.

I'll never know if the snake could have slithered silently into the house through the open window, or if it had frequently made its way along the ditch undetected and completely uninterested in our home. There seemed to be an unspoken collective agreement among the townsfolk that the mamba had to die. They were definitely in charge once the beast was identified. I supposed the risk was just too huge to allow its freedom to potentially threaten all creatures living close by.

Once home, I was happy to sit quietly in the living room with a cup of tea, my feet up as my funny parrot walked along the window seat, jumped onto my shoulder and put his head under my chin for a tickle. Thoughts wondered to the beautiful green mamba and the excitement it had generated. Quite absentmindedly while playing with Sparky's wings, I realized we both were contentedly purring.

14

Killing Me Softly

"I want to see no Red Cross, no Caritas, no World
Council of Churches, no Pope, no missionaries and no
UN delegations. I want to prevent even one Ibo having
even one thing to eat before their capitulation"
~ *Brigadier Benjamin Adekunle* [1]

Of course there were plenty of hard weapons used by
both sides in the Biafran war. What I learned about was
starvation: the equally effective soft variety of killing. A total
food blockade was the weapon the military government
deliberately used to destroy their Igbo opponents in the
Eastern State of Biafra[2]. And it was the children, especially
the babies, who suffered, took the brunt of the cruelty.
Adult humans can live without a daily meal of protein, but
babies need it regularly every day and throughout the day.
Babies therefore were so vulnerable to starvation.

From 1967 to 1969, with farmers off fighting; with fertile
farm land lost as war moved onto it; as fishing and cattle

---

1 US Office of Historian
2 The Biafra Story, Frederick Forsyth

sources of protein were lost, food sources consistently and precipitously dwindled. Complicating the problem was the increasing number of refugees flooding towns and villages throughout Biafra. Therefore there could be no organized food rationing, some black-market goods were available for those who could pay, but there was no substantial subsidized program for babies and young children as there had been in the UK in 1941. My mother had been issued a government ration book allowing her to purchase a strictly controlled weekly grocery supply for the two of us. There was nothing like that in any part of Biafra.

The embargo on food had been in place since 1967 when war started. Ironically, in the early days of 1969 there was some food available in Calabar but not in the north of the State where borders were strictly controlled, the embargo strictly enforced[3]. Destruction had smashed its way through Calabar two years earlier and the remaining community of traumatized, yet resourceful residents had subsequently rallied to make arrangements to secure food. For instance: they might have had food trucked in from neighbouring Cameroon; or arranged for boats to drop food off on a beach to the south; or have friends leave food beyond the southern borders of Biafra. The Igbo people were smart problem solvers and they found ways to avoid any dangerous exposure to federal fighters. But

---

3 Wikipedia

to have access to any entrepreneurial source of food they had to have money. And with the continued huge influx of refugees into Calabar, there wasn't enough food to satisfy that increased demand: refugees were starving.

I was lucky enough to give a pilot a shopping list whenever he flew the small Fairchild Hiller helicopter to Lagos on a beer-run, he took Margaret's list too which she found very helpful. On my deux chevaux, I found I could rely on small shops scattered about the town, as well. Now I wonder, as I write that, if I might have deprived local people access to canned and dried goods I purchased there.

Within Calabar, aid agencies did their best to make food available at designated locations like the refugee camp or the small hospital where a caravan kitchen, serving some kind of mysterious porridge, would arrive at a parking lot or a clearing in the trees. Women would line up, their bowls ready, while their children sat waiting in a tree's shade. Often the taste and texture of the mush served was so foreign it could not be swallowed. Imagine being offered a mixture of reconstituted dried cod, stockfish, beans, rice, corn and dried milk powder, donations from well-meaning countries who gave what food they had in abundance. Remember, the Igbo diet had never included milk.

To give birth is the start of a long saga of responsibility for any mother anywhere. Consider a mother whose partner is dead, injured or away fighting; or a mother with several children to care for; or a mother caring for children of her dead sister, brother; or a mother with responsibilities for elderly parents, her own, her partner's. Who knew how complicated family responsibilities might be. The addition of another life to care for was frequently just too much to take on.

I learned this while volunteering at Calabar's small rural hospital, a collection of quonset huts in the bush.

One hut for babies, was staffed by Igbo nurses trained at Guy's Hospital in London, a pillar of medical education and care in the city center. I knew it well and could talk to them about their time there as students. These nurses were strong, capable and knowledgeable ladies, with big hearts and endless love for the new lives they cared for. They worked with patient persistence even though resources available to them were meager and the demands enormous. When we stopped at eleven o'clock for a cup of tea, as was tradition at Guy's, they would share their exhaustion and sadness with me, their irrepressible dedication shining from their lovely, tired faces.

The walls of this hut were lined with metal cots, once white, now greyed enamel, worn and damaged, their long sides collapsible for easy access to the mattress. A quiet place. Babies placed two or three across a cot had no energy to voice complaint or need, their big black eyes stared into desperation. Oh, how cruel it was. There were so many babies and no cotton bedding. Naked babies laid on red waterproof sheets pulled tightly across the mattress: a harsh contrast to the womb they had recently vacated. An overhead fan attempted to keep the hot, humid air moving.

So busy and exhausted, the nurses and I bathed and fed babies as part of our morning routine. I was encouraged to hold their tiny bare bodies over my shoulder—their skin damp to my touch. We coo-cooed to them, hummed and sang to them, whispered nurturing nothings to them, smiled and loved them all.

At home, I shortened my two floor length dresses and cut the long sleeves off my two blouses to make little front opening vests for the babies, sewn by hand at every free moment during the days and nights after all the entertaining was done and visitors were on their way to their beds somewhere in Calabar or in our home. It was a small gesture that gave me some satisfaction, but who washed them?

What really shocked me was how many babies died during the night. When I arrived on my deux chevaux bike in the mornings, I knew babies were missing, the occupants of cots were changed. I couldn't understand how or why babies would disappear. Eventually the charge nurse calmly took me for a walk in the bush nearby. It was lunchtime and a mobile kitchen had set up under a tree.

She told me that the war, starvation, and hopelessness made life so desperate for women about to give birth, that often they would deliver their baby in the bush. I was stunned. She pointed to a track heading into the trees. 'Someone coming along that path to the hospital would find the newborn lying there and bring it to the ward for us to look after. The mother, with no support, her breasts dry perhaps from feeding an older child, perhaps from a lack of nutrition during her pregnancy and fearing that her baby would die because she couldn't care for it, would deliberately give birth and leave her baby on a piece of fabric where someone would find it and bring it to the ward.'

So that's what was happening. I was horrified. The rose window of Rouen Cathedral flashed into my memory as a reminder to take a deep breath and let go of the ache in my heart.

'That is why so many babies are weak, hungry and sick when you come in the mornings. They have been exposed and neglected instead of having received protection and care.'

I understood. Of course with all the love and devotion the staff provided, it was never enough, and it was often too late.

———

At about that time, a visiting journalist who was staying with us gave me a black and white photo he'd taken at the hospital. In the foreground, a young child, a little boy I think, perhaps two or three years old, squatted in the shade. Behind him, a line of ladies waited to have their bowls filled at the mobile kitchen, one lady had turned her head to look at him. The child's huge belly rested on his lap, skinny arms just hung at his sides. His large expressionless eyes stared directly into the camera, his face empty of interest, his thin hair already quite grey, his legs, bony sticks too weak to support him to stand.

He was the child I'd heard and read about. The desperate Biafran government had used similar photographs to awaken the conscience of the world to the plight of their country and their children in a desperate plea for help. I hadn't seen any children in Calabar with such advanced protein deficiency disease. Until this photograph, which said it all. This little child was the perfect picture of Kwashiorkor syndrome and a metaphor for the horrific murderous effects of starvation.

———

Those mothers, those babies, torn apart by war, haunt me still. I now know what happens in Ukraine, Yemen, Sudan, Gaza--wherever war is raging on the planet. I know that babies continue to pay the price with their demise. These were enormous lessons for me and I wondered if I'd be able to continue tolerating the pain and sadness of losing so many babies day after day. There was no respite. How could I turn my back on innocent lives, how could I not? It was an existential nightmare for me.

15

'De Enemy Dun Cum'. A Tribute to Jacob

How did he find us, Jacob, our houseman?

An ageless gentleman whose surname I never knew. A willing man of level disposition, uncomplaining, reliable, perhaps a little older than me. Initially he helped out in the flat, the first home Terry and I shared after leaving the Federal Palace Hotel in the spring of 1968. Up one dark flight of concrete block stairs. The building had no redeeming features, except that's where Jacob found us.

From our first meeting at the door of the little flat in Ikeja when he came looking for a job, there seemed to be an intuitive understanding between us. It was Terry who had the conversation with the person who became our houseman. Although I wasn't privy to Jacob's story, I concurred with Terry's decision to take him on. Jacob would anticipate my needs in small ways, especially once we were living in Calabar, when my days spent with the babies or refugees took a toll on my spirit, there was always a cup of tea ready for me when I arrived home. He willingly took on tasks he must have found quite strange, like saving scraps of wax paper, paper bags and candle runts to be reused, little behaviours I did as part of my post-war mentality.

To answer my question, I have decided that Jacob found the two of us while we were still living in Lagos. Conversations around a hotel dinner table can place the speakers in a sort of spatially protected togetherness. If Jacob had friends working as servers at the hotel, they would have access to conversations without looking as if they were eavesdropping. He might have heard the conversations in person. When the mention of towns in Biafra came up they would pay discreet attention, then pass the news around to friends who wanted to get back to their Biafran home; these were chunks of information, long shots worth remembering, because life could be dangerous for Igbo people living in Lagos. It was strange that Europeans there knew nothing about the most terrible war playing out in the north, central, and eastern provinces of Nigeria. But I bet the Biafran people knew exactly what was happening.

Months before the helicopter mission became a reality, Jacob had appeared to ask us for a job, and Terry must have foreseen the benefits of employing him there in Ikeja because he'd be useful to help me when I was alone with Terry off flying somewhere. Jacob's shopping lists were written in an educated script and with a biblical name like Jacob, he was Christian. Definitely Igbo, he belonged in

Biafra. He and I eventually traveled together in the back of one of the H-34s on the last leg of the epic helicopter ferrying. I was heading into another unknown adventure in Calabar, Jacob escaping to the safety of his people.

From early June 1968 until the beginning of October that year, I was employed as an occupational therapist at the Nigerian Armed Forces Rehabilitation Hospital in Lagos, enjoying working while Terry would often be away for weeks at a time. So, without my own car and driver, having Jacob around to do shopping, washing, and cleaning, I felt quite indulged, and without realizing it, having a houseman was the only solution to my being alone in Lagos.

I traveled back and forth from the flat on the northern outskirts of the city to the hospital in its center by van, provided by the facility: the last person to be picked up in the morning and the first to be dropped off at night. For convenience and because I was the only white passenger, I had been directed by the driver to share the front passenger seat, sitting close to the door. From there, when the vehicle was stopped at a roadblock, I could quickly scrunch down, which I had to do several times, under the dashboard, be covered with bags, sweaters anything handy, while the gun toting policeman walked around the vehicle waving his weapon in the air and shouting questions at the driver. It seemed that war gave policemen extra liberties. Finding a white woman would have created an awkward situation for me and the driver. How would he explain when he really didn't know why I was traveling as his passenger?

———

Many of my patients, young soldiers of the federal army fighting the Biafran people, were not well-trained soldiers. I had the impression they'd been quickly forced into uniform after being made to sign up to fight. They weren't educated or worldly. They might never have previously left their village or been employed or been injured. Issued a weapon, courtesy of the UK or Russia, they were expected to use it to kill. Could they know they were fighting the Igbo people for their high-quality oil that had recently been discovered under Biafra, oil the President Yakabu Gowan claimed to enrich his federal government?

Having lived with the British military system for most of his life, Nigeria's new president and head of the military, knew how to manage an army. His was well organized, comprising divisions of soldiers led by trained, capable officers. It wasn't a rag-tag organization, but the young soldiers from small villages were very different to the professionals who had graduated from military training schools such as Sandhurst in the UK.

My young patients had been wounded on the front lines. Their initial injuries were stabilized in a field tent; followed by a long, hot journey by ambulance to this hospital in Lagos for more treatment and rehabilitation if needed. Full of fear, bewilderment, and pain: separated from family, village, and by language, there was so much they could not understand. They might not have grasped that successful rehabilitation would mean being returned to the front lines. Those who did understand saw the only way to avoid that outcome was to be dismissed. But how?

Many of my patients had self-inflicted wounds to hands or feet.

To engage these young soldiers, an Indian physiotherapist and I had to be creative. In the early days, our patients laughed at us and refused our attempts at real rehabilitation. We knew young men had been in the army long enough to respond to commands from male officers which neither of us were. We needed a soldier attached to our small, two-person team, someone who could also translate our instructions into various dialects/languages, and we needed a well-equipped, air-conditioned room. If someone in the Army thought that therapy services were necessary in a rehabilitation hospital it was surprising no-one in administration had any knowledge or experience of how to make the idea work. Perhaps having a rehabilitation team supported the name of the facility, but we alone couldn't work magic or miracles.

I mentioned my frustrations to Jacob.

He suggested 'Voodoo'. It sounded very unprofessional, but being desperate, we gave it a try. The idea Jacob helped us come up with was simple. One that involved plenty of movement the young soldiers would not associate with exercise. First, we had to engage the sergeant, our soldier. He agreed to explain our instructions which must have seemed harmless enough to him. We told him that we were using an African type of rehabilitation especially suited to treat wounded soldiers. And if anyone wanted more information, we'd use Jacob's idea of having questioned a medicine man who advised the following, for example: 'Go barefooted to the stream, hop across the large stones to the other side, squat down with toes in the mud, pick long grasses, weave a headband, hop back on the rocks, give the headband to our officer, wash and dry feet.' The sergeant would put a check mark on a successful soldier's record and the following week we'd have some other cleverly planned movement activity. It worked. Gross and fine motor, balance and self-care, all good rehabilitation goals and our patients never suspected a thing. Maybe we *could* work magic. For older and more seriously traumatized patients we used traditional interventions, always with the sergeant translating our directions. Where would we have been without Jacob and his clever idea?

———

Everything changed at the beginning of October when I resigned from the hospital. I was eager to go with Terry to the Olympic Games in Mexico City followed by a trip to Canada for my brother's birthday and to visit some of my friends in Quebec and Ontario who wanted to hear my stories firsthand. After that chance meeting with Robert Robards, Terry was preoccupied with planning, organizing and preparing the UNICEF Relief Mission. He needed Jacob for as long as we stayed in Lagos, but once the two helicopters were purchased in Tel Aviv, Terry had to be with them to assure all Israeli markings were removed, which crept into November. So Jacob found a home for himself in Lagos and waited to hear when he could join us at Ikeja airport for a flight to Calabar. That took till mid-January 1969.

———

When the Relief Mission was finally established in Calabar, war was to our north. After each long day, Terry and I were frequently joined by visitors; some were officials from Lagos or other Nigerian towns, some connected with the United Nations, some associated with the International Red Cross teams. Conversations around our supper table were all about which destinations the helicopters had visited; how much weight they had carried; and how many round trips they had made. There was curiosity about what the Red Cross staff were up to (did they sell their jeeps?) and which cargo ship was expected in the harbour carrying what supplies and who was the captain?

Ships' captains were integral to the success of the mission and some of them were extremely generous by inviting us for a meal on board, meals we couldn't get in Calabar: quality meats, sometimes fish, fresh vegetables and fruit, wine, chocolate, hard alcohol. We would be sent home with a leg of lamb to roast, a plump chicken and a couple of bottles of good reds. We entertained them too at our home and Jacob got to taste some treats. His vocabulary might have expanded as the wine disappeared and voices were raised.

We all were living under extreme pressure because, in addition to being on this isolated edge of a civil war, our support was becoming more and more unreliable. Terry worried every day about how he would pay the bills for helicopter fuel and maintenance, wages for the crew, food, and most importantly, beer. Finding enough money was becoming a challenge as Mr. Robards' plans and promises were more and more questionable. If he was being paid by UNICEF and the federal government, why was it so difficult for Terry to have what he needed to keep the mission operational?

Following Calabar's destruction prior to our arrival, there no longer were guest houses or hotels available to accommodate those frequent visitors from Lagos and abroad. They stayed with us. We kept two spare bedrooms ready at all times. I'd have been lost without Jacob. He managed the washing (there was only a wringer, not a washing machine) and the housework; I looked after the shopping, cooking, and planning. The longer we worked together the more efficient we became. He epitomized the Igbo character of diligence and reliability.

I remember in the very early days of managing the house together when a UN official stayed with us. He had descended the steps of the DC-3 with his butterfly net raised in anticipation of a successful hunt. A display of priorities that disgusted me, but Jacob, perhaps recognizing the man's importance, was more polite, as was expected of him.

During the meal that visitor shared with us, I suggested Jacob serve the food through a hutch, a rectangular hole in the wall between the kitchen and dining room, a feature I'd never previously encountered and had no idea how to use. I made a total hash of my instructions, because, Jacob managed to place the casserole dish onto the sideboard by passing it through the opening, (not handing it to me, but placing it himself on the sideboard, an amazing feat of balance and coordination), and then he tried to climb through the opening to begin serving. I managed to rescue him before he got stuck or put his elbow in the stew. Neither of us understood how the hutch worked. If only we'd rehearsed the procedure. But would that have been helpful? Probably thinking my request quite ridiculous but willing to do what I had suggested, Jacob agreed with me never to use the silly hutch again. It was my 'ah-ha' moment of understanding how easily my instructions could be so misinterpreted and a moment we both were able to laugh about together. There was no flicker of amusement or comment from the butterfly man. I was glad to see him return to Lagos.

Looking back, Jacob might have had previous work as a houseman, he seemed to know what to do, but I was utterly ignorant and felt we were always working things out together. Our worlds were very different.

———

It was Jacob who, time after time, saved Sparky when the parrot jumped out of the ground floor window; and on a night we could have been bombed, it was Jacob who ran from the Palace up the hill to warn us of danger. Inside our front door he switched off the outside and hall lights and shouted as he climbed the stairs two at a time, *'Douse de lights, de enemy dun cum'.* Terry put his book away.

Jacob joined us in a dark corner of the balcony. We heard a deep rumble. The sound of a plane approaching, a dark shadow sliced the moonlight. This was serious. Spell bound, we watched the slow approach of an old DC-3 as it made a U-turn pass over the house then followed the road down the hill towards town. We saw someone toss a box of what could have been a type of Molotov cocktail from one of the plane's open windows; the ensuing loud explosion created a huge crater near the airport runway. Very bad timing if the 'gift' had been intended for us.

A quick run down to the Palace reassured the three of us that the helicopters were parked and intact on the playground, George the Cow was safe in his pen of oil drums, the building untouched. Pilots and housemen had gone to their beds, sure the excitement was over. We called goodnight to Jacob as he opened the Palace's front door and thanked him for running to warn us.

How had he known?

Deep in thought Terry and I silently climbed the hill to home. And then a chuckle, Terry was wondering if the 'gift' had been intended for our home and if the pilot of the DC-3 was one of his friends. I chuckled too: if Jacob had been warned and the pilot intentionally missed our targeted house, it was possible we were in very good hands.

I found out by reading Terry's biography more than forty years later, that the mercenary pilots flying old DC-3s were in fact working for the Biafrans, operating a gun running operation at night that the federal army brass wanted to curtail. So it was possible for the pilot to make a slight detour, fly over our home as if seriously going to drop the 'bombs' on us. And it was possible that Jacob was told to warn us by that same friendly foe. With strange allegiances at play, anything was possible. This was a clever plan that worked: Jacob was safe, we were too, and the pilot would continue on his gun-running assignment, with no harm to anyone. Terry understood it was a warning.

───

For about seven months during the spring and summer of 1968 and for a nine month period in 1969 Jacob was part of my every day while I was in Nigeria, his congenial willingness helped me so much. I trusted him. When we took over the house on the hill, there was no key: it didn't seem to matter. It created a *laisse faire* approach to our home. Friends would knock on the door with an 'Hello' and just walk in. If they waited, then Jacob would answer the knock and make a decision to let them in or call one of us. For his own entrance, he chose to use the back door. As the man of the house, Terry knew about Jacob's past, his goals. I never questioned him about personal information, I could see he knew what behaviour was appropriate. Just quietly working together, without a lot of discussion but with a huge amount of gratitude, we became friends.

16

Exit

One very hot and humid, late summer Sunday afternoon I joined the crew for a swim in the river we'd heard so much about. I imagined tree-lined banks and bubbly clear water. Not this river.

When we hopped into an inflatable dinghy provided by one of those generous ship captains, and someone pushed us away from the bare, muddy shore, we were swept away by a soupy brown current into a floating assortment of debris: a lonely old black sandal, a ragged grimy under vest, a child's punctured blue ball. And a naked body spreadeagled in rigor mortise. They all floated bumpety bump down to the sea. How many hundreds of bodies exited the country that way, disappearing into oblivion?

For months I had stubbornly chosen not to, but with that experience, had to accept the close proximity of war. I had a quick dip rather than a real swim. During the chaotic dash back to the craft, with oars flailing to turn it around, my head must have been splashed, because, within hours, pain in my vulnerable left ear exploded, followed by swelling and red-hot pulsations. Then a discharge that reminded me of the chronic ear-ache episodes I'd experienced as a child during the other war. That terrible pain. While the crew enjoyed a celebratory, rare day-off meal and happy conversations at the Palace, I withdrew alone into a dark corner of the front porch to rock and sob uncontrollably, not able to muster even enough energy to feed George, my precious young cow.

Terry quickly realized this severe ear infection was much more than the goodies in his first aid box could tackle. Rather, it warranted my immediate evacuation to *Montréal* and the doctor who had helped me with a previous ear drum emergency. So while I packed my few belongings, Terry organized my transport from Nigeria to Canada. Once that was complete I climbed into the small helicopter and we set off for the airport in Lagos. There was no time for goodbyes to Margaret and the children or thank yous to Jacob and the crew at the Palace.

But Africa wasn't finished with me. In Ikeja airport's crowded, noisy departure lounge, I needed to borrow a pen from an immigration official who got chatty. Leaning towards me on his lectern-like barrier with an open smile that showed his beautiful white teeth he probably thought I'd find irresistible, he threatened to prevent my departure unless I agreed to go out with him. Despite the screaming pain in my ear, I promised to do that - on my return. Pleased I had managed to outsmart him, I would normally have written off the encounter as a bad joke, but this time it was a burdensome addition to what was a deeply emotional exit from the Biafran State I'd grown to respect.

As it turned out, the moonlit Molotov raid was a harbinger of profound changes for the UN Relief Mission in Calabar. In spite of its huge success, operating helicopters without reliable financial support could not be sustained. The situation continued to deteriorate as Mr. Robards deliberately manipulated the truth, cheated, schemed, and squandered. When he was caught, identified, and charged, the federal police gave him a month to leave the country and that applied to everyone working with him. Anger erupted from the decent Biafran Minister of Rehabilitation and other administrators when they received news that the mission, which, by delivering more than 2,000 tonnes of food to the war torn north and saving thousands of lives, was ending. It was another blow to their valiant fight for autonomy.

While all the shenanigans had been carried on behind the scenes, I certainly knew there was something terribly amiss. Snippets of conversations came my way, but I couldn't have imagined the extent of the catastrophe that ensued in spite of Terry's best efforts to keep the mission functioning.

In a strange twist of timing, my sudden infection forced my departure before the weight of the police came crashing down on Mr. Robards and his entourage. I was relieved to know I wouldn't be a liability because, by the time Terry and the pilots organized their own safe departures, I would be a far-away memory.

———

The three days and two nights it took me to arrive in *Montréal* were a blur of long flights and endless layovers I cannot remember. But I do recall the relief when I saw my dear father and brother who rushed me to my old ear, nose and throat doctor at the Royal Victoria hospital. It took the doctor a week to identify the rare equatorial bug and another to acquire the correct antibiotic treatment. As a precaution, I had to wait in a lonely, isolation room with plenty of time to recover from jet lag, regain strength, and think about the life I'd left.

Were Terry and the crew safe from the tug of war going on between Robert Robards, the federal government, the Biafran state and federal police? I imagined that with Terry's help his crew would manage to elude those officers of the law whose interests were focused on Robards. But how and where would they escape? Through Cameroon? My great heartache was not having any way to contact our friends and housemen after leaving without a goodbye.

What happened to them: our loyal, kind Jacob, Wednesday, Friday and Sunday? Did one of them adopt my young cow, or did George end up in someone's cooking pot as I feared? And Sparky, who had cheered all of us up after hundreds of fraught hours spent dedicated to the Biafran cause. What happened to him? There were never answers to these questions.

In my sterile confinement, I heard on CBC radio news that Biafra was suffering increasing defeats, Umuahia, its main town, had fallen and many smaller towns, too. The spoils of this war were going to Nigeria, Britain, and the Soviet Union: oil--for which one and a half million (perhaps more) Igbo people died, trying to protect it, themselves, and their state.

Eventually, when my doctor was satisfied that I was no longer a threat, he discharged me, and on that happy day I began to share with my family and friends these stories I'd accumulated over two years traveling in Africa.

What about Terry? As long as he had managed to escape, I knew he would be busy searching for the next adventure, perhaps one I'd look forward to also?

I waited for a letter.

PART THREE

Hiatus

17

Few Weeks after Calabar

Love recognizes no barriers. It jumps hurdles,
leaps fences, penetrates walls to arrive at its
destination full of hope.

~ *Maya Angelou*

He escaped. The letter I received was sent from Bangkok, where he had a stopover on his way to another war. This time in Laos. How had he orchestrated this move, from one war-zone to another in such a short period of time? He would be flying for Laos Air Charter. The letter contained an invitation for me to join him, tickets were included to Brussels and Bangkok. His 'oh, by the way' instructions to me were to 'stop in Brussels and pick up an envelope from Mme. Troget,' one of his Kinshasa friends I'd heard about but never met.

I did go to see her.

From my hotel in the center of Brussels it took three buses to reach Mme. Troget's home in the suburbs. She greeted me with a cheery 'Bonjour' and bisous, the cheek kisses shared between family and friends. She spoke in rapid French about Terry: how was he, what was he doing? I was sure she knew exactly where he was and what he was up to. Her living room, where we sat for coffee and a chat, was an African fantasy land with two huge elephant tusks framing a black brick fireplace and a zebra skin under the coffee table. She was cordial and, of course, curious. It was what she didn't say that made me realize all the innuendo. She had a secret.

At last, she reached into her pocket to pull out a small, white, padded envelope with my name on it in Terry's writing. This was why I'd been sent to meet her. She told me to put the envelope in a safe place and only open it to read Terry's message when I got to my hotel room. Of course, I couldn't help fingering it and noticing a lump. Oooooo. Then I was back on the buses, fiercely holding onto my back pack with the envelope safely inside till I got into the dark, little hotel room downtown, my turn to be full of curiosity. The simple instructions, which I read immediately, told me to take the contents to a jeweler in the city, have a ring made to fit, then proceed to Bangkok.

At this point I felt a little nervous panic and remembered the old trick of wedging a chair under the doorknob (when I was chased in Venice) and closing the window blind for security. Then sitting on the edge of a rather dingy bed, I poured the contents of the envelope into my palm. There was the most beautiful jewel I had ever seen or touched. Like the sun shining on water, it shimmered with brilliance and rainbow colours in the light of the bare overhead bulb. I couldn't take my eyes from it. I might have gasped or moaned out loud. It was such a wondrous moment, yet I was experiencing it all alone.

I hardly slept for frequent checks on the diamond back in its envelope under the pillow. Early the following morning, I took my precious gem to a shop I remembered visiting near the Grande Place and gave the jeweler the instructions from Terry's note. He took an immediate interest in the diamond, weighing it (1.8 carats), examining its perfect clarity and pure colour, trying to identify where it came from: South Africa? I had to confess, I didn't know, but I could see how impressed he was with its perfection. During the two days' wait, I returned to my old favourite walks, coffee shops, the Atomium, and gardens in the 1958 World Fair site, remembering how this romance had begun.

From time to time the subject of marriage had come up during that last fraught year together in Calabar. There was no proposal, no long candlelit supper culminating in the offer of a ring—nothing like that. The essence of a wedding was in the ether, a vague intention, not verbalized but inferred that we would marry someday.

Then, there it was: a simple solitaire diamond in gold. I was thrilled to collect it and, under the jeweler's watchful gaze, I put it on my ring finger in his shop. He might have given me a hug as he held the door open for me to walk out into my future.

18

Laotian Interlude

I had traveled alone to Bangkok, old Siam.

After collecting my backpack from baggage claim, I was whisked away from the airport by a smartly dressed Terry. Although it was only a few weeks since I'd left Calabar with an infected ear, it had been years since I'd seen him in a suit and tie, looking quite dashing. He immediately examined and gave his approval to my ring that still delighted me with its beauty and significance, significance he acknowledged but wasn't comfortable talking about then. (I had learned to trust his actions rather than his words.) Having been in possession of the ring for less than twenty-four hours, I was still learning to be nonchalant about wearing it, it was so eye-catching sitting there on my left hand. And every glance reminded me of what I had personally and privately agreed to, by accepting the diamond as a proposal... What had I agreed to? With my eyes wide open, I agreed to accept this man I loved, all his many foibles and his strengths, for better and for worse. My life had taken a ninety-degree turn I was just beginning to understand.

After a surprise celebratory dinner with friends and an overnight stay at a posh hotel in downtown Bangkok, we took a taxi through almost solid, morning traffic all the way to the airport for a flight to Laos. Terry's luck at jumping from one job to another had worked again. He would be flying fixed-wing aircraft and I understood, by his lack of enthusiasm as he explained, it was a job, nothing more than that; a job he would tolerate for as long as necessary.

We were based in the outskirts of Vientiane, the capital, close to the well-known and not-so-mighty Mekong River, several hundred miles north of its famous delta. The house we found was small, with tiled floors, not unlike the floors in the Palace in Calabar, suitable in hot climates, especially if there were cows, or dogs in the household.

Soon there was a puppy. Terry couldn't resist a purebred Doberman, about six weeks old, he named Goris, and insisted on having the dog's ears cropped according to American Kennel Club rules. What was he thinking? I protested but the surgery went ahead, and it fell to me to spend nights on the cold floor beside the puppy to prevent him from scratching off the dressings and tongue depressors supporting his ears in prefect symmetry. What a cruel procedure. After the wounds healed, I was pleased that one ear refused to stay upright. It flopped up and down as we ran along the river. Some mornings on those runs, I would see four large water buffaloes, solid-looking creatures, peacefully cooling their hooves in deep pools. Recalling that their African cousins, if threatened, were known to charge at terrific speed, Goris and I slowed our pace and gave them plenty of space. Wild animals, what a treat.

Street food! Lots of it in Vientiane. Quick, delicious, and entertaining; the cooking taking place in large woks on wide sidewalks with dramatic stirrings and loud calls by the cooks to passersby. We soon found favourites to enjoy on our cool evening walks along Vientiane's Champs-Elysée-like broad main road. My usual choice was a Laotian variation of Mongolian BarBQ - thin slices of beef with lots of fresh vegetables in a hot, spicy sauce. I would be drooling in anticipation as we approached the cook. We'd take our plates and sit on a bench to eat as we watched people and cars cruise by, Goris pleading for a forbidden nibble.

A short walk from our cottage was the Lang Xang Hotel, a popular gathering place, especially for expats and journalists. We often stopped there after our evening picnics. One Sunday morning in late September 1969, we decided to try it for the breakfast we'd heard about, taking the last two empty seats at the bar. A small, intimate room with about eight two-person tables along one short wall,

all the tables occupied by people deep in conversation, their heads nearly touching. Catching a word here and there we realized they were all representing a cross-section of the world's news reporters, sharing their latest stories in English. Terry had to explain to me why their conversations were so intense: because they were reporting on two nearby parallel civil wars, the Secret War no one outside Laos talked about, and the Vietnam War everyone talked about. I was fascinated to watch the furtive glances over their shoulders as if they were surreptitiously, seeking, comparing, or confirming information they'd heard, perhaps all three. The determined force of their discussions, which was hard to ignore, interested Terry, so we made a point of breakfasting there every Sunday to catch snippets.

It didn't seem to matter where in the world I went, there was often a friend or two I'd known from the past and Vientiane was no exception. This time it was Michel, a chef we both remembered from South Africa who, having married a Laotian, Su, made his home a few miles north of town. Their house, built on top of a gentle slope with magnificent teak trees dotting the landscape and a wall of thick bamboo flourishing along the driveway, provided long views above treetops to far away hills, every inch tree covered and beautifully picturesque. Su called her antique shop 'Su's Antics' which was a good pun that amused me, until the day we were invited for a visit, and I saw what antics Su was up to.

Terry and Michel had been keeping in touch, but we hadn't seen him since our trip to Cape Town four years previously we had lots to talk about, including the significance of my new diamond. We were happily chatting when we heard Su shouting in Laotian outside. Did she need help? Was this one of her antics? Yes, it was. Looking over the balcony we saw her, a hammer in her fist, striding to their car, still screaming. Then smash, smash, smash, the headlights were gone, glass flew in all directions leaving two hollow orbits where lights had been. Hoping to distract her, we called to her, but it didn't work. She wasn't finished. Marching around to the back of the car, she took her anger out on the rear lights too.

I would have enjoyed a walk with her around the garden with its jackfruit, lychee and mango trees, but Su had disappeared. Michel, obviously distraught, was not surprised by her behaviour. She was known to be highly strung. Her country was at war, presumably she had fears, unreasonable fears that made her angry. Or was she jealous of Michel's friendship with us? We all were willing to speak French to appease her, if that was the problem. Eventually, we thought it best to reschedule our catch-up-with-news meal together in Vientiane, later.

Sadly that didn't happen.

Our stay in Laos passed slowly, I wasn't particularly happy and apart from my reliable Goris, I hadn't made any new friends. Access to Su was limited and Terry was still not satisfied flying fixed-wing aircraft. The job was boring. He needed to get back to helicopters, and a quick search of chopper companies advertising for pilots struck gold. There was a job available on Kauai, one of the Hawaiian Islands. After a brief phone call, he wrote a new resume, sent it by mail to Kauai, and I began to feel the possibility of escape from this beautiful but disturbing country. Another move I greedily anticipated, this time with a clever and handsome young dog.

As we waited, Terry received an invitation to a party at the home of one of the directors of Laos Air Charter; this time, it included me. I hadn't been to a party since the unforgettable event in Port Harcourt, Biafra, with the soon-to-be *Medicines sans Frontiers*. I wondered what this one would be like. The bungalow was twice the size of Michel's, similarly situated in the country, surrounded by gardens, sculptured lawns, large and lovely Frangipani and African Tulip trees and clumps of bamboo. A veranda wrapped around the house with wide spaces connecting to inside rooms; the party hub focused on the living room, made even larger by its windows having been slid out of sight. Very clever. There was a well-stocked bar, music, a couple of people dancing on an outside terrace which was so lovely with yellow and pink plumeria and begonias growing in large dark-blue glazed pots. But even in this million-dollar setting, there was no laughter, only whispers.

While I took it all in, Terry had been swept away. I didn't see who took him or where he went. Wanting to, but unable to tag along with him gave me uncomfortable feelings of being out of place, until I was asked to dance, and then I knew I was out of place. But, *better*, I thought, *than sitting on the sidelines*, where I'd been heading. The music was slow, my chubby dance partner held me too tightly, wasn't much of a dancer, and I could see then that Terry, deep in serious conversation, wasn't going to rescue me. So when my partner whispered in my good ear in French: *and what do you know?* my discomfort suddenly exploded and I promptly excused myself, gave Terry a look that said *I've had enough*, and moved towards the door.

Who were these somber people? Where was the joy? Could they all be stressed-out pilots and associated co-workers for the Charter Company? Was it a party to cheer them all up? Why was I set up, by being asked to dance and then asked that crazy question: *what did I know?* About what? Was it a game?

Strange feelings had haunted me since my early days in Laos as Terry told me stories of people he flew taking dangerous chances lightheartedly; Su's obvious discomfort; the reporters we saw deep in discussion over the news they were hearing; Terry making it clear he wasn't happy flying here; even the water buffaloes were possible threats. And then Mr. Chubby's accusatory question in French. The intrigue was doubtless due to the close proximity of two serious civil wars in which many powerful international performers had roles to play. After only a few weeks in Vientiane, I'd noticed an undercurrent of something going on I didn't understand that seemed to threaten my well-being in some way. My normal, everyday stress was being boosted to an uncomfortable level. Having been trained not to ask questions or expect explanations from Terry, I decided to put Laos behind me, to look forward to living on an Hawaiian island, in America.

Because Hawaii required months of animal quarantine, and with our departure imminent, we asked our friends to take care of Goris. He was a smart and careful puppy, might he befriend and reassure Su? Although I felt an ache in my heart every time I thought of leaving him, I sincerely hoped our decision would be a good fit for us all, especially me, as I was already imagining Goris spending his days running freely in Michel and Su's wide grassy garden under those exotic trees.

19

Australia? Absolutely

The next step was to an American paradise, the beautiful island of Kauai with jobs for us both: Rehabilitation Specialist for me and flying helicopters for Terry, with no war and nobody starving. It was the perfect place for a wedding.

Which we had, in March 1970, in the old stone church with my Dad, his wife and our few mates cheering us on. Standing with us was a new friend, Mary Jasper in her hand-made pink cotton dress, and Bob Billings, Terry's best-man.

After four wonderful years on Kauai island it was time to move again this time to Somerset West, South Africa where our child, Roger, was born in 1975, my 34th year.

Although I had been swept off my feet when I first met Terry, the future really did bring many quite wonderful surprises, adventures I couldn't have imagined: like flying the length of Africa from Nigeria to Cape Town in a small bright red Bell helicopter, call number 007: day after day skirting waterfalls, thousands of wild animals, the jungle tree tops. Or while living in Cape Town, learning to fly a small, fixed wing Cessna, until my Afrikaner teacher's hand crept under my blouse as I executed a steep climbing turn, putting me off learning to fly with him. Or being volunteered by Terry, to evaluate camping facilities at 'Chobe', a soon-to-be-open Game Park in Botswana with my tiny five month old baby who slept through an event that continues to thrill me. Woken by a scratching noise nearby, I saw the tent material undulating and felt something firm brush my arm from outside the canvas wall as an enormous elephant slowly plodded past us.

And when Roger was eight months old, Terry changed employment again.

We found ourselves next in Bardufoss, northern Norway, where the long summers of midnight sun followed by months of chilling darkness frustrated and motivated me to find some weather I could understand. But before I found that place, one afternoon near Spitsbergen on the Svalbard archipelago, we drove over the frozen totally flat, white permafrost in an 'icemobile' (my term). The three of us huddled closely together in a tiny, windowed cab, and watched the animal nonchalantly lumber ahead of us. It wasn't as huge as I'd imagined, more rounded and cuddly looking. Once we stopped, it calmly turned to look back and we saw that handsome face with its coal black eyes and nose, its presence both frightening and fabulous. We held our breaths. Baby Roger, only nine months old, was as quiet as a falling snowflake. Unfortunately, he doesn't remember that thrilling experience either. But I will never forget how my dream of seeing a polar bear in the wild became reality.

Searching for somewhere sunny finally paid off, which meant leaving Terry alone to continue to brave the complexities of life above the Arctic Circle. I chose to go to Australia, since I was qualified to work there, and it was summer! With return airline tickets to Melbourne in my backpack, we decided to have one more adventure together traveling by train from Bardufoss to the Ilsa de Capri in the Bay of Naples, legendary home of the sirens, (mythical creatures part human, part bird with irresistible voices, introduced by Homer in his poem the *Odyssey*). We neither heard nor saw them, but it was fun to look and listen for them. Ten days of walking, exploring, and yes visiting the Famous Blue Grotto by boat, provided a grand send off. When we returned to Norway, I was prepared for the next chapter of my life.

With one medium sized suitcase, baby Roger and I flew west from Oslo over the British Isles, across the Atlantic Ocean,

North America, and the Pacific Ocean to Melbourne in southeastern Australia where an occupational therapy contract awaited me.

Roger enjoyed four birthdays there in comfort with communities of friends, first in Victoria, then Queensland. Australian summers and winters were tolerably familiar to me as was language, culture, and my employment, so I decided to stay until Terry found work in a more acceptable climate and environment.

But I never expected that eventually he would announce: The Kingdom of Saudi Arabia as the place where we'd reassemble our little family.

British Pavilion hostess at *Montréal's* World Fair, Canada 1967

Joan and Terry, week-end sojourn at a Laurentian lake,
Province of Québec, Canada 1967

Jacob, delivering joy. December 1968

George the Cow lying in the shade of UN 007
(Fairchild Hiller), Calaber, Biafra, Nigeria, on the
'Palace' playground 1969

Kauai, Hawaii, USA March 1970

Very old window with once elegant fretwork,
Jeddeh, Saudi Arabia 1980

Joan and four year old Roger, spring holiday Bardufoss,
N. Norway 1979

View from 4th floor flat, Saudia City, Jeddah, Saudi Arabia,
looking westward to a desalination plant and Red Sea 1981

'Oval with Points.' Joan's friend, the huge bronze sculpture
by British artist Henry Moore located on a Jeddah round-
about on the *Corniche*. Saudi Arabia 1981

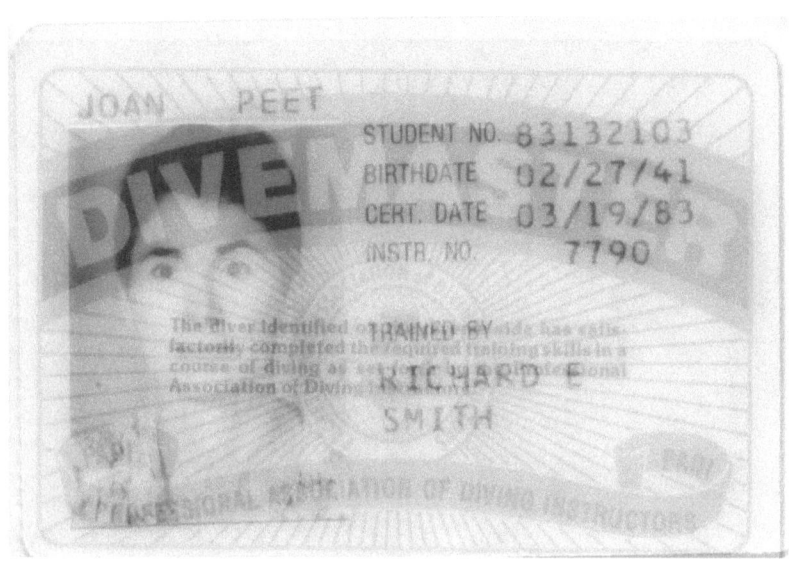

Joan–a PADI Divemaster

PART FOUR

A Kingdom at My Door

PART FOUR

20

So This Is Jeddah

A couple of months before my contract as occupational therapist in Coffs Harbour, Australia ended, Terry had taken a job in Jeddah, on the eastern shore of the Red Sea. He would be flying helicopters for Saudia Airlines. His passengers, American, United States Geological Survey (USGS) personnel and French, *Bureau de Reserches Géologique et Minières (BRGM)* geologists, contracted to explore the Kingdom for alternative treasures to oil.

———

By1979 Saudi Arabia was exploding with growth as oil dollars created a vast spread of wealth across the land. Jeddah, being the main port, had to grow remarkably quickly to accommodate huge changes.

Historically, from 350 BCE to 1850 CE, Jeddah occupied a densely populated square mile of coast around a natural harbour protected by a strong wall with a substantial gate across the road to the Muslim holiest town of Mecca, forty-five miles away to the east. Once the Suez Canal was opened in1869, it was inevitable that worldwide traders discovered the old town of Ash Sham. Within the next one hundred years, the ancient, protective walls came down allowing Jeddah to emerge into a bustling city that spread north and south along the coastal plain and eastward into the desert. The ancient center still exists as the old Suq, dwarfed now by modern, baby skyscrapers of steel and glass, constantly droning motorways, and all the accouterments of the 21st century.

By 1979 when Roger and I joined Terry, the population, along with its cars, had burgeoned to such an extent that city planners took drastic measures to solve the massive parking problem. Substantial reclamation of the coral reef foreshore was required on which to build adequate parking facilities near the city center.

A desert city of a million residents and host to hundreds of thousands who annually visited to participate in the Muslim pilgrimage of the Hajj required plenty of reliable and secure water. Hauling it by camels across the desert from distant wells would no longer suffice. Water was eventually piped from Wadi Fatima, fifty miles to the south, and when that was no longer adequate, the supply was augmented by desalination plants.

With space in the city so limited and so valuable, lovely historic homes were selected for protection after careful evaluation and refurbishing if their construction was sound. If other old buildings, no higher than palm trees, had to be demolished, then some sort of construction project was immediately ready to move onto the site. It was building mania. Only on reflection do I recall the many cranes dotting the city skyline in 1980 as buildings were growing twenty to thirty stories high. There were dozens.

———

What I knew about Jeddah when I arrived was hardly complimentary. From Australian friends I'd learned that although Saudi Arabia was extraordinarily rich, it was in no way welcoming or hospitable. Rather, the country was closed to foreigners, without any tourism. Its serious religious and royal controls were absolute. The long list of rules intended to protect Islamic values included no alcohol consumption, no Valentine's Day red roses, special mandatory outdoor black clothing for women, no pornography, prohibition on women driving, no movie theatres, and no single women in public unless accompanied by a man to whom she was related. There were many others. Women were seen as protected and men as prevented from temptation. There was to be no mingling of the sexes, even the lines for food at McDonald's restaurants were separated by gender.

As guardian of the Sunni faith and one hundred percent Islamic, Saudi Arabia tolerated no religious icons or services of any other religion although small meetings in private homes were acceptable. Israeli passport holders were not allowed into the country and people entering whose passport had an Israeli stamp were refused. I made sure my removable Israeli stamp was not in my passport when I entered the country. Saudi Arabian visas were required for entry into the Kingdom, to purchase a ticket to leave, and for legal employment within the country. To me the rules seemed extreme, they affected all aspects of life, and any unintentional or intentional infraction could and did lead to very serious consequences: imprisonment or deportation. The rules, applied to everyone regardless of ethnicity and nationality, contributed to the reason my Australian friends warned me to expect life in the Kingdom to be a hardship posting.

Roger and I finally landed in Jeddah quite refreshed. It was July 1979.

Long flights from Sydney, Australia, to the Kingdom of Bahrain were over. We'd slept, played games, swum, and read during our three-day layover in its capitol, Manama, waiting for our visas to arrive at the Saudi Embassy. Then one more flight across the desert to Jeddah and our happy family reunion.

Then what? I'd heard about the flat in Saudia City that came with his contract and expected to go there, but instead Terry took us from the airport to a house in an American community of geologists where he was housesitting. Those typical large, split-level, 3-bedroom buildings, with sliding glass doors opening onto grassy gardens full of flowers and trees, were right out of *Sunset Magazine*. In his latest letters, Terry mentioned how much he was enjoying housesitting, but he hadn't described the compounds and their beautiful homes, and he hadn't described the Saudia flat either.

When we arrived he was staying in George's home, one of the geologists in 16 House Compound which, along with 8 House Compound, were two gated communities, home to the United States Geological Survey personnel. The compounds were islands of Americana located across the very busy north-south dual carriageway, the *Corniche*, from the American Embassy. Although Terry was provided with the flat as part of his employment contract with Saudia Airlines, by frequently housesitting for the Americans when they had to leave to do field work or make trips back to the States, he, and by association Roger and I, inherited a second set of homes. These scientists and support staff became our extended family, our community.

Across the driveway from George's house was a family exactly like ours with a Mum and Dad and a young son Paul, only a few months younger than Roger, both boys heading for their fifth birthdays. Their friendship was immediate. It took me a few days to realize this wonderful arrangement was a temporary, although frequent occurrence, and that between housesittings we would have to return to the Saudia City flat. In the meantime, we settled into this new reality and loved it. Our introduction to all things Saudi Arabian couldn't have been more cordial.

Perhaps indicative of Terry's prowess was his ability to befriend a community of English-speaking professionals with diplomatic privileges who, as part of their contract in that dry, austere land, had alcohol allowances and access to a commissary, movie nights, and lots of great parties. An Olympic-size pool became a welcome destination with a swim team Roger was invited to join. He swam for the American School at a meet in Cairo when he was only five years old. Waving him off with his teammates and coach was a memorable maternal challenge, but he returned jubilant from his first solo international adventure. Perhaps the beginning of an irrepressible travel bug like his mother's.

It didn't seem much of a hardship posting to me. So far.

Within 16 House Compound I could walk around as if I were at home in the UK or Canada, but to venture beyond the protection of the gated wall I had to wear what all women wore: an *abâya*, a black tent-like cloak that covered me from neck to ankles, and a black head covering or *hijab*. Mine were silk. Both required by law, both very sweaty, never mind that Jeddah, on the 22nd parallel, was an unbelievably hot, humid city. Having known freedom to choose what I wore in public, I confess to initially feeling miffed by having to conform to the clothing requirements imposed on Saudi women, until I realized how important it was to identify with them by covering myself from top to bottom in black also.

Saudi men wore the traditional *thobe*, a long white caftan-like garment. They covered their heads with a red and white cotton scarf called a *kaffiyi* (it reminded me of a French cafe tablecloth) held in place by a black cord called *agal*. Non-Saudi men could wear western style clothing.

Drilled into me from day one as representing compliance with the Saudi regime, was the importance of the dress code. Sleek high-heeled shoes were frowned upon as being too sexy, so I wondered how slim Philippine Airline stewardesses I saw shopping in the mall got away with wearing them and tight jeans and not much in the way of cover. They were either living dangerously or perhaps had the protection of a Prince. I was warned if I tried to imitate their fashion, it would be my husband who'd suffer consequences because of his inability to control me.

I have mentioned social rules for Saudi women based, I thought, on fear and a need to control, but men also had to obey rules. A man in public could only share the company of a woman who was his mother, daughter, aunt; some female family member. As I spent more time in Jeddah, this rule had potentially serious consequences for me, since I wasn't allowed to drive and often needed a ride from someone not related to me when Terry was away flying. Many of our English friends working in the port without the company of their wives were willing to help, and to them I was truly indebted. I thanked them with invitations to share many home-cooked meals, grateful that no one was ever caught, punished, or deported for their assistance.

Roger and I arrived in Jeddah to find that Terry had not only discovered the Americans and been befriended by them, he'd also found where to purchase life's necessities. There were two sources of food: the vegetable suq and Leb Joe's grocery shop (where all the fruit juice cartons had the word *Juice* blacked out. Sounded like *Jews*?). Terry would drive us, but when he was out in the desert for days or weeks at a time, one of his dock office worker friends would step up to be my chauffeur if I chose a time convenient to them. The volunteer then acted as my chaperon while I did my shopping, completely covered in black silk.

The vegetable suq was a vast, cluttered chaos of huts, tables, and boxes. Tissue paper and plastic littered the potholed earth on which narrow tables were lined up in some sort of order each supporting an assortment of vegetables grouped together by types in wooden frames, all outdoors. English greengrocers also display their produce on shelves outside their shop's front windows. But this suq, using a similar arrangement multiplied many times by quantity and type of produce in colours, shapes, tastes, and origins I didn't always recognize; was a fascinating trip around the world of vegetables. In the large vacant part of the lot, hundreds of patrons left their cars haphazardly parked, pointing in any direction wherever there was space. No neat white lines indicated order.

Leb Joe's was organized. Like a mini-super market, all the different departments were under a roof, not the same roof. A rambling warren of specialty sections had been added onto the original rustic building over the years. There were Housewares: Chinese steamers, woks, dish clothes hanging at eye level, piles of plates, glasses, pots and pans. Hardware: hammers, spades, screws, cans of paint, ladders. Clothing: long racks of colourful *caftans*, the type preferred by Saudi ladies, clothes for babies, children, *thobes* for men. Groceries: all sorts of food items from around the world, in refrigerators and freezers, on shelves that wound around and around the small rooms from near the floor to near the ceiling. *Hawajiis* (strangers) with diplomatic passports shopped at their commissary, but everyone else I knew depended on Leb Joe's. This store, representing all the cultures and cuisines existing in Jeddah, was a huge melting pot of food. Consequently, the variety was international, but one item not available was liquuor-filled chocolates. Regardless, I began to explore the international opportunities.

———

Of all the countries I had lived in prior to 1979, this was the most difficult to understand. Taking its social policies on board as a way of life certainly was burdensome for me, as my Australian friends had suggested. Saudi social structure, so deeply influenced by a combination of belief in the Sunni faith and the ruling principles of the royal family, was challenging, but I intended to do my best to find peace while living with them.

21

Letting Go

The news blurted from the young man standing on the doorstep took my breath away. Overwhelmed by shock, I didn't recognize him or think to invite him in from the blistering heat. I just stood in the open doorway at 16 House Compound in a fog of dismay. Fortunately Terry came to my rescue by joining us to greet the man by name and invite him inside. He was the young English mechanic with the Saudia helicopter operation. They started to chat. But wait, had I misheard? I rudely interrupted their conversation: 'Did I hear you correctly...has the bag with all my jewelry been stolen?' Tears began to build behind my eyelids, my lips trembled as a warm flush spread through my whole body. Oh no.

During the first few days following my arrival in Jeddah from Australia, and while we were housesitting for George at 16 House Compound, I had met this young English man, I'll call Derek, but I hardly knew him. On the last occasion, he mentioned that he was planning to go to Bahrain to be married, his fiancé preparing to fly from England to meet him in Manama, the capitol city. I remembered how excited he was as he told us about their plans: they were going to stay at the Al Jazira Hotel. This was interesting.

Roger and I had stayed at the Al Jazira until our Saudi Arabian entry visas were ready for us to pick up from the Embassy. Anticipating a two to three day stay at the hotel, I'd put my little black patent leather bag containing my jewelry in the hotel safe behind the reception desk. With an excited early morning rush to get to the airport for our early morning flight to Jeddah, I'd left it there.

Closing up our Australian home in Coff's Harbour, Queensland, saying *Good Bye* to friends and workmates after four peaceful and productive years there, had been exhausting both physically and emotionally for Roger and me. After more than forty-eight hours in planes and airports, we added jet lag to our fatigue, and those three lazy days of waiting allowed us to recover and relax: swimming in the hotel pool, loafing in the palm trees' shade, reading and playing games. I had no need for jewelry as three days flew by.

—

My little black bag held a profusion of treasures, some sentimental: my 21st birthday pearls and one personal favourite: a heavy gold charm bracelet I'd created since arriving in Canada as a twelve-year-old, each silver or gold memento linked to a tangible memory. First, a ballet slipper for the fledgling dancer I was on Ile Bigras, a *Montréal* suburb, then a pair of skis, a canoe. As my world expanded with travels across Canada, my summer holiday visits to Europe, birthdays, graduation from McGill University, so did the weight and worth of the bracelet. With its many links occupied with one or two charms, it was a unique record of my life. Valuable too.

Most precious were gifts to my mother by my dad on his return from naval action in the Mediterranean after WWII. One was an antique heavy gold chain necklace with a substantial dangling pearl and my favourite: a narrow, carved bracelet of Egyptian designs in silver that held three large cabochon stones of exquisitely colourful and extremely rare Alexandrite that flashed purple/red, blue, and green. Compared to my mother's prewar cherished 'diamond' engagement ring, sparkly, but made of glass, these two pieces were precious indeed.

Having been in Jeddah for about four weeks without any clue how to retrieve my jewelry, and with no plans to travel to Manama in my foreseeable future, Derek provided a solution I hadn't anticipated. It seemed fortuitous. Should I trust him with my treasures? I decided to go ahead and ask him to recover my bag and return it to me. I wrote a letter of authorization he could present to the hotel management and the bag would be handed over to him. No problem.

But there was a problem. It had just occurred when he returned to Jeddah.

Earlier in the morning Derek had phoned. He wanted to deliver the bag to me as quickly as possible, and now that he was home, he needed to buy food. Since the vegetable suq was on his way to 16 House Compound, he would stop there first to do his shopping and 'See you soon.'

In innocent anticipation, I waited for Derek's knock on the door. Then eagerly opened it to learn the stunning truth. Still feeling shocked and broken, I lead the way into the living room to hear his story: he left my shiny bag on the back seat of his old car when he went to buy vegetables and when he returned with his purchases, the bag was gone. As simple a story as that. Could it have fallen? Had he searched under the seat? Yes, yes, it wasn't there, and there was nothing he could do in such a busy marketplace, he understood the perpetrator could have been anywhere. So, as a well-behaved Englishman, Derek hadn't shouted for security, or made a huge fuss, or slammed the car door in fury. No. I also knew that wouldn't have helped. As his story unfolded, I saw the futility in pursuing the matter, not wanting to believe my jewelry was gone, it seemed to be true. Yet I felt I couldn't just let the matter go.

Robbery in Saudi Arabia was serious, I had recently learned the punishment was amputation of one or both hands. In spite of that very real deterrent, an opportunist had taken my bag from the back seat of a quickly parked car among hundreds of others.

What to do? Contact the Saudi Police.

Derek would not allow my precious possessions to be stolen and immediately come knocking on my door with a phony story, would he? Was he upset by what had happened? Did my distress accentuate his feelings? I couldn't tell. He reminded me while we were waiting for the police, 'that robbery was punishable by...' and the rest of the sentence was lost when they arrived.

But we both knew.

I told two policemen the story as it had been told to me, expecting they'd want a description of the stolen items in case they turned up in the gold suq or pawn shops (without knowing if there were such shops in Jeddah).

They had another idea. By turning to Derek to ask his name, address, and employer, I suddenly realized that he had become the suspect. That idea had crept into my thoughts too, I confess, but if I allowed it to go any further, the consequences for Derek might be life changing in a bizarre and debilitating way. How would I feel about such a possibility? With that thought in mind I had to accept my loss. and sadly try to let it go.

That's the nature of robbery, it's cruel, selfish and greedy. Accepting Derek's innocence for my peace of mind, I had to have faith that someone would benefit. But at that moment, I had a hard time believing that that someone could be sitting across from me in George's living room.

———

Letting go of hurtful thoughts is difficult. Even now, more than forty years later, I occasionally wonder why Derek had handled my bag so casually when he went to buy vegetables. Why didn't he lock the car, close the windows, take the bag with him? Had I been too hasty in giving him my trust? Why hadn't he thought to visit the vegetable souq after making sure the bag was back in my possession?

Perhaps he and his wife had looked inside the little bag and decided the contents would make a special wedding present. She could have placed the bag in her suitcase and returned to England with it, as I had tucked it into my backpack many times. Derek could come back to Jeddah without the goodies, make up the vegetable suq story and no-one would be the wiser. It might have been a perfect crime.

Whatever the truth, I was never again to enjoy the contents of my precious black bag. I never heard from the police, and I never saw Derek again.

22

Matawa in the Market

Roger and I had traveled from wintry Australia to an extremely hot and humid summer in Jeddah, and because we were housesitting for George in the American compound, we had the pleasure of its Olympic-size swimming pool to lounge in all day if we wanted to. Young Roger and his new friend, Paul, were getting up to all kinds of fun and games together, proof that Terry's friendship with the Americans turned out to be a very fortuitous liaison.

By September, our parental priority was to find a preschool for Roger. Since we were a British family, we quickly contacted our embassy and Mrs. Pagaela was recommended. Her little school for five children in her home suited us perfectly. She was a keen English lady breaking the rule of needing a work visa to be employed. I respected her for that and for her enthusiasm in teaching our son to read, spell, write, and draw before his fifth birthday. Roger had started right away and really enjoyed going to school.

We liked Mrs. Pagaela. We thought she'd be a suitable first guest to try out our entertaining skills since Terry and I had been living apart for four years. On the phone, when I called to invite her, she said, 'I want you to know that we don't eat cheesecake.' OK. She knew we were British, so I don't know why she associated cheesecake with us, it was more an American desert, perhaps it was just their preference to not eat it. I assured her: 'You're in luck, I wouldn't have a clue how to make it.'

She and her husband came to George's home in 16 House Compound where we were housesitting, both were easy going, our conversation flowed comfortably. The menu I'd chosen was our favourite: beef fondue, accompanied by pickled vegetables, potatoes, and broccoli. At the table with the herb-flavoured oil warming up in the fondue pot over a candle, long and regular forks in position beside the plates, I offered Mrs. Pagaela the bowl of cubed raw beef. Her look was one of surprise then horror 'Oh.' she said, putting her hand over her heart, 'I prefer to eat my meat cooked.' Poor dear, had we become British barbarians? Fondue had been all the rage in Australia, but it obviously hadn't reached Jeddah. I quickly explained. They both got it, and the meal progressed with enjoyment and laughter. They were converted. For years we continued to mimic her expression each time we served raw meat for a fondue. I still do.

Having lived in Jeddah for several years, Julie, Paul's mother, had made lots of useful connections. She knew her way around in more ways than one, and I was to benefit early on from her tutelage. She kindly insisted on introducing me to Jeddah. Our first foray would be into the Suq, the historic center of the old city, a stone's throw from the port, where, through its open doors, migrants, stevedores, adventurers, crooks, mafia members, good guys, and bad guys all entered to mingle in Jeddah's heart. Initially, I had some reservations about visiting the suq alone without speaking the language or understanding written signs and having no idea what to expect. So, Julie, with access to a car and driver, not only took away my apprehension but became my willing guide. I was very grateful.

My anticipation bubbled up under my new *abâya* and *hijab* when, with Roger safely at Mrs. Pagaela's, we headed off on an adventure. Sitting in the back seat of the car as traffic whizzed by was terrifying. Saudi drivers, recently freed from depending on camels for transportation, enjoyed harassing other drivers by nonstop honking. They drove with unreasonable speed, executed crazy zigzags, lurched away from green traffic lights, the worst driving behaviour I'd ever experienced (and that included French drivers). My palms had nail prints in them by the time we arrived at our destination, the only large department store and parking lot on the edge of the suq.

Telling the driver to return for us in two hours, Julie led the way. I immediately felt a magnetic tingle of excitement as the world I knew changed and all links to time disappeared. We approached the bustling pedestrian traffic and blended in. It was like traveling back four hundred years into narrow cobbled passageways that twisted and turned in unpredictable ways: crowds of men dressed in the national garb of long white *thobe* and *gutra* and dusty leather sandals; women of all shapes hidden under a black cloak *abâya* with a black *hijab* scarf covering their heads. Before we had climbed into the car at her home, Julie had made sure that I too, knew how to cover my clothing and head appropriately. I was learning how important these requirements were.

Impossible to rush, and I didn't want to. People were everywhere: sauntering close together, talking animatedly, stirring up dust as cobbles changed to sand, deeper along the paths. Everywhere I looked I saw something new. Little glass-fronted shops selling gold, I really wanted to go inside to take a long gaze at all the glitter and beauty. Tent-like enclosures filled with hundreds of bolts of material, some piled precariously high. My mind started to imagine how I could create long skirts, sewn by hand if necessary. Around a corner, exotic smells tickled our noses: the spice suq, an impromptu arrangement of barrels, displaying wicker baskets piled high with pyramids of powdered cumin, coriander, cinnamon, cloves. Of course, I wanted to take some home. Next the clothing tent: a three-sided lean-to of black canvas, with a ceiling of long dry, curly palm fronds providing shade, under which many black-clad women seriously concentrated on their decision-making. To my eyes all the sample dresses seemed to look the same: long sleeves, floor length, high neck, with surprisingly bright colours, intriguing patterns and lovely materials as if to make up for their monotony of style.

And always the heat. Heat that seemed to rise from the sandy ground filling the air with dust, as if we were walking through dry soup. I wanted to stop and shrug off my sticky skin, but Julie insisted I keep moving by pulling on my sleeve under the *abâya*. There was no escape.

I was having such a wonderful time looking left and right, avoiding pedestrians, I hadn't noticed the *hijab* no longer covered my head but was lying jauntily around my shoulders. Distraction was no excuse. I was guilty. For approaching me through the crowd lumbered a *Matawa*, a religious policeman. Julie and I abruptly stopped. He was an old, stooped, grey-haired man, under layers of faded black, well-worn robes, his leathery, lined face lacked any amusement and his eyes burned into mine with angry sparks. He smashed his long wooden stick between my feet into the dusty earth, gesticulating with his free hand while directing a loud, angry, garlic, and spittle-laden stream of Arabic at me. Without understanding a word, his message was clear, 'WHY IS YOUR HEAD NOT COVERED?' I was weak kneed, befuddled.

Julie, whose light-brown hair was also not covered, was ignored. I supposed that, with my dark hair and tanned complexion, he saw me as one of his flock. I stoically took the entire brunt of his venom into my pounding heart, carefully replaced the *hijab* as I had been taught, and with downcast eyes, meekly stepped aside. He made little growling noises as he shuffled off, accentuating each alternative step with a loud and meaningful crash of his stick as he went. That sound became integrated into my consciousness in all subsequent suq visits as a warning to check my presentation: head covered, abâya snugly closed around my body and no skin exposed anywhere.

The magic Julie and I had enjoyed vanished, replaced with relief, fear, disbelief.

And time was up. We soberly retraced our steps back to the waiting car. In accepting the Matawa's chastisement, I had also accepted his warning: I was a guest in that strangely disciplined country, my appearance was critical to my safety, and by extension, I must be aware of what I said. Suspicion entered my heart. Julie's friendly driver had ears, who knew where his allegiances lay?

We sat together quietly sipping our water in the back of the car, our private thoughts for company, each of us digesting what had happened, all the way home.

23

Settling Down

Housesitting for our American friends in their compounds during our first year in Jeddah was quite delightful. I think of it now as a kindness to us. But when the home's resident eventually returned and our assistance no longer needed, we had to return to our assigned flat on the fourth floor of a block of 16 units just inside the East Gate of Saudia City. Located about two miles north of our geologist friends, this compound was huge, walled, and filled with a hundred or so similar concrete blocks of flats housing an international polyglot of expatriate Saudia Airlines employees. There, roads were unpaved, the air dusty with hardly anything green in sight to brighten the drab, sandy landscape. Hardship quickly became more apparent, especially as we were separated from the friends and conveniences of 16 and 8 House Compounds.

I could walk to neighbours in Saudia City for support and friendship, taking Roger to play with friends, and an Arabic language class for me. Which I did, but oh how I missed my USGS second families I depended on for a social visit or a swim in their pool.

From our living room window in the Saudia City flat, we could look west over small homes to the Red Sea and one of the hulking dark, desalination plants at the north end of the *Corniche*. This twenty-mile-long main road and modern seaside promenade, of which the city administrators were very proud, was devoted to art and recreation. The latter of course, was the long stretch of beach; the art, international, prestigious and beautiful. Becoming more familiar with the city but increasingly more frustrated with the rules that weighed heavily on my shoulders, I was attracted to one piece of art: a massive sculpture of smooth polished bronze by Englishman Henry Moore called Oval with Points. It felt like a friend who understood metaphorically what the Kingdom was slowly doing to me.

As the months dawdled by, American friends encouraged me to join activities in the rather limited ex-patriot community. It took a couple of months and I did start to look at a variety of interests from the many I'd enjoyed before arriving in Jeddah.

The vast Red Sea beckoned me first to continue my fascination with scuba diving, a passion that bewitched me on the island of Kauai and never let go. Getting back into the water, so warm and welcoming, was an obvious next step.

Towards the end of 1980, I joined Jeddah Players, a group of theatrical enthusiasts who had been performing plays at Parents Cooperative School gymnasium for years. Although not interested in acting, I was happy to help by looking after props or stage managing. Only one hitch marred that memory.

It occurred after a successful performance on my fourtieth birthday, the one Terry didn't remember. The parrot I'd borrowed as a prop from a friend, with sincere promises to take special care of it, took advantage of its open cage door. In spite of my vigilance, yes, the cage door was open, and yes, the cage was empty. My loud wail 'Oh no,' brought a stagehand who pointed upwards 'Look, look.' Like all parrots, this one was responding to sudden freedom by flying in ever increasing circles, higher and higher, until it reached the gym's far off ceiling where it perched on a rafter.

This was serious. Although the shock I felt was momentarily ameliorated by remembering part of a childhood rhyme: '... aren't I glad that cows don't fly...' I had to trust the Yemeni janitor who stopped his sweeping to come to my rescue. By offering to lift the cage to ceiling level on his expandable platform ladder and leaving it there overnight, with food, water, and the open door, he promised me by morning the bird would be back inside. Hating to abandon the creature alone in that vast empty space after such an athletic flight, I left for home somewhat reassured.

Early the following day, I climbed up the ladder and there was the escapee, in his cage, with his eyes closed, standing on one leg, every once in a while stretching his wings in slow motion, one at a time. After topping up his food dish with a slice of fresh mango and giving his head a gentle tickle, I quickly closed and secured the door. What relief. Members of Jeddah Players were all delightful company, so who was responsible for endangering the bird and stressing me? I never did find out.

Since I had found creative ways to quickly cook up healthy meals to feed my family and the growing number of Englishmen from the docks depending on us for support and companionship, I was inspired to figure out how to turn my living room in the flat, into a cozy restaurant. Initially my plan was to offer a set menu for up to four persons on two late afternoons a week. The challenge was how to separately feed Roger, Terry, and those friends from the docks. Timing would be everything, as well as carefully planning which days to select for patrons. With our friends enthusiastically coming up with ideas, I realized by sharing their interests, we all were going to make the idea work.

But it never did. Fine print in the Saudia City Rule Book forbade any entrepreneurial undertaking within its compound. We all felt beaten, disappointed: it had been such an enticing idea.

With geology friends, outings were into the desert to camp and explore and with diving pals, trips were to distant beaches, both north and south, for aquatic adventures in more pristine waters. What could be better for exciting getaways than land and sea adventures? While housesitting, we sometimes ended the day with a swim in the USGS pool or watched a movie in 16 House Compound's community room. Was there ever a more normal way to end a day?

By being friends with Americans who'd lived in the city for several years, we couldn't help benefiting royally by hearing their many stories accumulated as they traveled to locations far afield across deserts on camel paths. We heard about their favourite places, some historic, some just interesting. Over the months I'd made a list of tempting adventures especially if Roger and Paul could go along also. I would be open to new discoveries, especially everything Jeddah and the surrounding desert had to offer.

With my new interests and a mental list to motivate my curiosity, I slowly started to settle down, more determined than ever to live as normal a life as possible in this country of rigid rules.

24

Unexpected Exercise

What kind of expectations for a happy Christmas did I have, living in a Muslim country?

My disappointment, when a custom official threw out my liquor filled chocolates at 'Arrivals' in Jeddah in July1979, foretold of many restrictions I was being conditioned to accept.

By the time December arrived, Roger and I had made a few decorations, from a two-foot-high paper Christmas tree to tiny felt bells, stars and angels inspired by pictures in an Australian magazine I'd hidden in the bottom of my suitcase. Without knowing if a ladies magazine was forbidden, I had taken the precaution of protecting it and am glad I did, only wished I'd thought of doing that with the chocolates. We used flour and water glue to make paper chains to hang across the front window at George's house and baked lots of cookies from recipes in the magazine, my only cooking resource.

Our first Christmas in Saudi Arabia found us housesitting at 16 House Compound again. With access to their commissary, the Americans had what it took to make a traditional holiday 'Merry and Bright', in spite of the absolute lack of anything Christmassy anywhere else in Jeddah. We enjoyed many parties, gatherings around the pool, and community dinners with our new temporary neighbours. It still didn't seem like a hardship posting.

When Roger graduated from Mrs. Pagaela's preschool in December, Terry, in one of his 'Oh, by the way' moments, signed him up to attend the American-run Parents Cooperative School (PCS). British children, like Roger, typically attended school at their embassy. There was never any explanation or discussion regarding his decision. Terry must have had his reasons.

Now that Roger had started elementary school, about half a mile to the southeast from the American compounds, we would walk there together along tidy, quiet residential streets and I'd be alone on the walk back each day. We had settled into a pleasant routine. With Terry off flying during the week, I discovered freedom, a sort of empty nest feeling. With my usual letter writing, sewing, cooking, and the huge pool, some days were full of activity. But, ready for a challenge, I couldn't help thinking about the possibility of finding a job.

Between 16 and 8 House Compounds was a large gravel parking lot used by the geology staff with a guard's hut at one end in the shade of a tall tree. Because I'd always enjoyed running in the mornings, I had the idea to use the empty space as a running track. Once the geologists had driven off to work, I had the lot to myself and by my calculation, by running from end to end one hundred times, I would have covered a mile perhaps more.

The friendly old Yemeni guard watched in amusement as I ran, my long skirt flapping around my ankles, less than ideal, but it was a safe and private place where I had no worries; no one advised me not to run. Rather, I enjoyed being alone with my thoughts in moving meditation. After that experience with the Matawa, the exercise helped me feel more confident and comfortable in the world beyond the compound confines.

One day Roger and I walked to school along the north-south road immediately east of 8 House Compound. The road was wide, with a walkway butting up to tall protective garden walls each overhung with colourful, flamboyant tree branches, like curtains shading the empty pavement. The teacher knew I was willing to stay a while to help her, then leave Roger happily busy and head back to our temporary 'home' in one of the compounds, secure in the knowledge that I was appropriately dressed, my strides brisk and bold along the sun dappled sidewalk.

Ordinarily, the street was empty of cars, empty of people. Ahead was a dark Mercedes sedan parked facing me, close to the curb. Its easily identifiable profile spoke of affluence, prestige and its closed, tinted windows of privacy. It wasn't there when we passed by earlier. Because the car's windshield reflected the bright blue sky, I couldn't tell if there was anyone inside, so assuming there might be a driver waiting for the owner, as sometimes happened, I continued my walk to the beat of Bee Gees music coming from the Walkman in my pocket.

Then, a feminine niggle of 'what if' suspicion suddenly prompted me to increase my speed. The tenor of my gait took on a firm 'don't mess with me' message, a 'Be Prepared' habit from Girl Guide days in Canada. About to pass the car's front passenger door, any composure I'd been holding onto disappeared when its window silently lowered and my automatic response was to quickly look inside.

Horrors. The scene was clear in a flash: the rotund naked belly, the flurry of agitation, the purple penis.

What to do? There was no other option than to run, the music in my ears ignored. Gathering up my skirt I had to run fast to reach the corner of 8 House Compound with its high walls and friendly gate guard. And I had to get there before the driver caught up with me, I could hear the screeching of wheels as he executed a U-turn in the empty road. The engine raced. The car was getting closer. Run! Reaching the unpaved, bumpy side road, I made a swift left turn close to the whitewashed adobe wall, then left again through the open gate and careened into the compound. There was no sign of the guard as I rounded his empty hut. Panting hard, I flattened myself against a sturdy tree trunk and listened. A car, slowing around the many potholes, continued down the road, past the gate.

Years ago, as a university student, I'd had a similar confrontation after leaving the anatomy lab alone one Sunday afternoon. The halls were dark and completely empty when a man in a long coat stepped out of the shadows and 'ta-da,' exposed all. That time I'd responded with a cool detached command, 'Put that thing away and get out, now.' And he did.

But this time, filled with apprehension and questions, I had immediately decided to run, without having any idea what consequences might have developed had I continued my determined walk. I might have given him the finger. The fear came from all the unfamiliar rules conditioning my thinking during my short time in Saudi Arabia. If I, an infidel without rights, broke a rule and was found guilty, it's possible my husband could be blamed and punished.

And why had this happened to me? As angry with myself as I was with the Saudi driver, it was the cunning, unexpected movement of the window, like the sudden swish of a lizard's tail in fallen leaves, that invited my reflexive response. Had he looked at me? Had I imagined a gloating glance in my direction to monitor my reaction and feed his ego? Was he an opportunist or a true deviant? I'll never know. It doesn't matter.

Saudi women never walked long distances alone: I was obviously a foreigner, so had to take some responsibility. Even with my suspicions aroused, I had fallen into his trap. This lesson taught me that feeling safe in the compound where I was hiding did not translate to being safe just a few steps away.

That evening Terry gave me lots of predictable advice: 'Stop being so damned independent,' an option I seriously considered. This scare had been totally unpredictable, I would have to be careful, but I just couldn't accept being reined in. I had to walk Roger to and from school while we were living in 16 House Compound, allowing him to walk by himself was unthinkable. There was no alternative.

After Thoughts

In combination with the strange laws I was learning to contend with, three memorable injustices contributed to my morbid feeling of 'victim' during my first few months in Jeddah.

Firstly, my jewelry was stolen only weeks after arriving. I hadn't realized what a consolation the contents of my little black bag were, how they triggered memories richly connecting me to my brother in Canada, and our deceased parents. Even though I didn't have jewelry to wear in Jeddah, I still remember how comforting my treasures were just having them within reach while I lived in Australia.

Within another couple of weeks, malice from the religious policeman during my introduction to the ancient suq with Julie, my temporary neighbour, shook my self-confidence. During that event in the suq, Julie and I had been correctly dressed before my *hijab* fell off. So he had the right to give me his personal warning. What hurt most was the unexpected venom in his loud and angry shouting. I wasn't used to that level of fury.

Had I invited the last ugly experience of unexpected exercise, correctly dressed but on my own? Was that the missing piece inspiring the Mercedes driver to taunt me? If a woman was required to be chaperoned by a man to whom she was related when out in public, then my solution was to stay at home which I totally refused to do. Now I knew walking alone made me vulnerable to danger, so I would have to be aware, careful and prepared. Now I knew there was no possibility of compromise between Saudi rules and my expectations, the problem became a seemingly impossible challenge, inviting frustrations and anger.

25

Back of the Bus

One morning, looking down to the East Gate from the fourth floor living room window in our Saudia City flat, I was surprised to see a full-size, single-decker bus, typical of the sort I'd ridden in rural communities all over the world. It took a few minutes to put on my *abâya* and head scarf and run down the four flights of stairs to check it out. But the bus was gone. Imagine my surprise when I noticed a sign on the wall indicating a bus stop, in English! Public transportation only minutes from my flat. It was the north terminus turnaround.

By taking an exploratory ride one early morning, alone in the very back where the ladies sat, I quickly learned the free bus traveled around the nearby ungated residential communities, then headed south along the *Corniche*, the busy motorway into the city, the suq, and to the department store. Unfortunately, it drove past 16 House Compound without stopping. I couldn't get off to cross the road and visit my friends. There were no stops until it reached the city. Getting off at the parking lot south terminal, I took a short walk past the department store windows and returned to hop into the back of the bus again for the return ride to Saudia City East Gate, still the lone passenger. I suspected that intentionally allowing women to get on and off the bus only at designated stops created a chaperon effect, controlling their liberty, very clever. Regardless of restrictions, to me the bus potentially represented limited but precious independence and I was determined to take advantage of all options.

———

A great hardship, and a fact of life in Jeddah at that time, (1979-1983), was that ladies were at a huge disadvantage by not being allowed to drive. Unless they had their own car and driver, all women legally depended on male members of their family for transportation and yes, they could use the bus if a route was accessible to their home.

Besides Terry, my other driver options were his friends (which meant breaking a law); hire a car and driver (expensive); contract with a taxi service (which we did once a reliable driver was recommended); walking (potentially dangerous but I could have Roger with me), and the bus. The bus was safe, reliable, free and legal, though not very frequent and not very comfortable, but I could not take Roger with me. There was always a 'but'.

Indeed, discovering public transport service from Saudia City East Gate, a very short walk from our building, was a charm.

Unique to buses in this Muslim country was an opaque barrier that completely separated the back third of seats from those in the front. A gender separation hangover from the days when most men didn't have cars and had to rely on the bus, or a camel. That had largely changed by the early 1980s. Very few men were without a car, almost none, and I don't recall any men occupying the large front section of the bus while I was a passenger in the back.

Those five double-bench seats were the ladies' domain. Even on busses, gender discrimination was blatant and might have contributed to the slow dawning of Saudi women's wishes for more independence. They were given the vote in 2011. But the desire to drive their own cars seriously began in early 1990 when several very brave activists protested, at the risk of losing their freedom. It would take another twenty-eight years for them to find strong, rational voices the royal decision-makers no longer ignored. Permission to drive was finally given in 2018. A transition which wasn't easy or comfortable. Old traditional guardianship laws continued their influence and the majority of women, especially those living outside of Riyadh, the capitol, continued to rely on their male relatives and the bus to get from place to place.

In those twenty-eight intervening years, was there a slow evolution to modernize the back of the bus? Did the barrier come down giving ladies more space? Were the old rattly, hot, and wretched vehicles replaced with comfortable air-conditioned coaches, because, in 1980, the only inside air was fume-filled, humid and hot, coming from high, narrow open windows. The ladies I traveled with didn't seem to be unhappy traveling around to do their errands in considerable discomfort. On the contrary, they showed me how resilient and accepting they were and as a veteran bus user, I was happy to join them.

———

During my student days in the early 1960s in *Montréal*, busy rush-hour buses were so packed with passengers sitting, standing, holding onto straps for balance, closely squashed together, that stray hands could easily wander. We quickly learned to give a well-placed elbow into the offending body, then let the incident go. Saudi bus arrangements created tranquility unheard of back then; although the space at the back was crowded, no one was groping us. Grateful for the safety and convenience the bus provided, I certainly didn't mind riding back there where some Saudia City acquaintances refused to join me because they felt it was demeaning. It wasn't. For me the bus was a godsend.

With Saudia City East Gate a terminus, I would be the first passenger on south bound and the last off on the return. I'd give the driver, probably a man from Yemen, a wave before climbing up the three steps, find a seat by a window and settle in for the slow meander around houses, the driver stopping to pick up ladies as the bus made its way downtown. I could tell by the way these shoppers grabbed the handrail to labouriously pull themselves up the steps, one at a time, that most were middle aged and not very fit. Some were plump, filling out their abâya, some were rather scruffy ladies, some exceptionally smelly under all that black in the heat and humidity. I found my bus mates charming in spite of weather-made challenges.

As they sat down and their *abâya* slipped open a little, I enjoyed peeking at their skirt material, they obviously loved bright colours. Although they weren't affluent, their clothes and shoes were a statement I could read about who they were and the choices they made. Occasionally I would see wealthy women step out of a Mercedes sedan at the department store, one leg and then the other, sporting elegant shoes and a flash of fabulous material that spoke of designer labels from London, Paris, and Rome.

In such a small intimate space at the back of the bus, we had to be friendly. I got to know several ladies, although not by name, whose scheduled trips to town coincided with mine. We were quiet, thoughtful, and polite leaving home in the morning, greeting one another formally with *'Marhaba,*

Kayf halik?' ('Hello, how are you?'), a smile and not much chatter. When the bus reached the narrow city lanes with their lovely old mansions, and I was allowed to alight, I'd give the ladies a wave and leave, preferring to walk in the shadows before doing my errands.

The atmosphere heading homeward was completely different. With our shopping done we'd meet at the city terminus and, if it looked like a wait was inevitable, have a tiny cup of espresso coffee standing in the shade of the kiosk, where an enterprising Yemeni gentleman sold the best sweet cardamon brew and crisp almond cookies. Back on the bus again, the atmosphere was relaxed. Fatigue from the heat and busy shopping didn't discourage loud and excited conversations I found so entertaining. They'd chat about their shopping, the heat, the crowds, the traffic, the bargains like ladies everywhere. I would join in with my few Arabic words, it was fun and they were helping me learn their language.

We pulled special purchases out of our bags to admire, and some treat to pass around as we headed home. I liked to offer nuts or sugared ginger cubes from white paper cones, sticky dates wrapped in brown paper from the old suq, and my favourite nougat, the ubiquitous chewy Mediterranean candy wrapped in rice paper. Chewing gum, figs, and a kind of pretzel, crunchy bread snack were popular offerings from the ladies. Occasionally our attention would be drawn to a most amazing pile-up of cars and all conversation would stop as we watched in disbelief. And always the constant honking of car horns.

I happened to be on the bus when it drove around a stately tree lined square of homes with a large open space in the center, usually empty of traffic and people. This time, an enormous crowd of men in their white *thobes* were milling around a small, raised stage on which three uniformed officials stood. Because I couldn't actually see what was happening, the ladies, noticing my quizzical look and realizing it was no use explaining in words, rallied to help me understand by acting out their explanation charade-like and I immediately saw the significance. Punishment for theft was to have one or both hands cut off, and this was the place and the occasion where those sentences were meted out in front of an audience of hundreds of men. My stomach did a somersault.

Realizing the event's gruesome significance, my thoughts had flashed back to 'Derek', the name I unexpectedly cried out loud, as I remembered the young man in whose possession my precious jewelry bag had been stolen. My decision not to pursue the investigation with the police had saved him from this terrible fate. Silence filled the back of the bus as it left the square. I'd seen enough. The old laws were really quite cruel.

Looking from one lady to another, studying their expressive faces, was the therapeutic diversion I needed at that moment. I could easily see that these women, having grown up with the guardianship laws didn't consider them terrifying. They were not oppressed. They were the boss of their family, they made decisions within their home. I could tell from their noisy, chatty sharing; their laughing, teasing pride; their nurturing, confident bearing; that they accepted their circumstances. And they accepted me. I felt included by smiles on their round, black framed faces and their easy eye contact.

They spoke quickly with a Jeddah accent that wasn't part of the language course I was taking in Saudia City. Remembering how bravely I had used hesitant French as a 12-year-old newcomer to *Montréal*, and how that had given me the confidence to just speak, I decided to use the same process with Arabic. It was working. But learning to speak Arabic from a textbook was impossible. What helped was for the ladies to teach me the names of our shopping items, our clothing, the days of the week, numbers. Conversing was impossible, but, in spite of my inability to use verbs and other parts of speech, we communicated using nouns, some verbs and lots of facial and body expressions. Attempts at practicing my growing Arabic vocabulary often generated huge guffaws at my surprising mistakes, but I really didn't mind being laughed at, I just joined in. Those bus rides with 'my lady friends' as I referred to them later when recounting the day's events at home, were healthy distractions for me in their lightheartedness.

———

One by one, as the bus zigzagged through networks of their residential communities, the ladies left the bus with a *'Fi Aman Illah'* ('God be with you'), carefully negotiating the three steep steps backwards with their heavy bags and a wave. Then alone in the back, I'd watch as the bus cruised beside the Red Sea beaches, north along the *Corniche* motorway with its extraordinary pieces of art, gave a nod to the Oval with Points until, driving around a Prince's almost empty lot, the bus stopped at the Saudia City East Gate for me to get off.

Another wave to the driver and I was through the gate, happily heading home.

26

Breaking the Law Again

I needed a job.

After Roger and Terry left for school and work and if I had no plans to visit friends in 16 and 8 House Compounds, and no errands to run, I was marooned in the fourth floor flat.

I really needed a job.

How could I find one without a work visa? I'd started to nibble my lips.

Amazingly, as if my plight was recognized, a request for occupational therapy help came by letter from the Bobath Center in London, where I had studied Neurodevelopmental Treatment (NDT) for cerebral palsy. I was invited to treat a young girl living in Jeddah who had recently been discharged after a couple of weeks of therapy at the Center. Having no idea how I had been discovered, I was delighted. The letter included names and a phone number, which I called and was put through to a woman who spoke English. Without hesitation, as if she'd been expecting my call, she arranged for a driver to pick me up and take me to the family home. Had the Bobath Center vouched for me? What good fortune.

I was going to be treating six-year-old Aminah, the daughter of a Saudi businessman, in her home. The child was cared for primarily by her unmarried aunt, her mother's sister, the lady I'd spoken to on the phone. On my arrival, it took no time at all to be warmly greeted and swept upstairs to Aminah's large room with lots of space for all sorts of movement: mats, therapy balls, toys to manipulate, and games. We would be working on self-care skills, ambulation, balance and eye-hand coordination.

No-one asked to see a work visa.

It was through the family's hospitality that I learned so much about how Saudi's lived and played, not so very differently from families all over the world where a child was the focus of their attention. It became part of the routine once the therapy session was over, for me to share a meal with Aminah's mother and aunty. The home's formal dining area was behind closed doors, a permanent private room for the family's use which probably was furnished with a large, low table and floor cushions. But for visitors like me, instead of using a table and cloth or place mats, servants carefully arranged newspapers on the huge, soft Afghani carpet that filled the home's spacious front entrance hall, where we ate, sitting on the floor.

A strange but perfectly accommodating arrangement. I was learning.

Bowls and plates of food had already been placed onto the well-organized newspapers when the three of us took our places on the carpet. The food, however, looked and smelled so inviting: always some sort of cooked, well-seasoned meat or fish, spiced, I learned, with a combination called baharat. This iconic Middle Eastern taste I introduced to my own cooking and continue to use, is a combination of freshly grated or ground cloves, nutmeg, cassia bark, cumin, cardamon, coriander, black pepper, and paprika. Mouth wateringly delicious. Rice was often cooked with pistachios, spices, onions, and raisins. Bowls of olives and raw vegetables and always baskets of white flat bread and soft, brown bread sticks were there for the taking. All homemade. Soda pop was their preferred drink.

We chatted amiably as we sat on the floor around the food, Aminah's aunty coming to our assistance when her sister and I, both with rudimentary knowledge of each other's language, got stuck. As the weeks passed and our familiarity grew, these ladies took pleasure in showing me some of their favourite possessions: shoes, jewelry, and delightful long dresses. Some just took my breath away. They weren't boasting, rather sharing and I appreciated seeing their treasures. Except for my shimmering diamond I wore all the time, I had nothing to compare, so I told them about the countries I'd visited in Africa. With due respect to this Muslim family, I chose not to tell them about my time in war-torn Biafra and hoped it was a fair exchange.

One day as we ate lunch, they told me stories about a recent family visit to an Ethiopian wedding which I subsequently replayed vicariously over and over in my thoughts, acknowledging how enjoyable it must have been, the loud and rhythmic music, dancing, fabulous food. Celebrations continued through the night and all the following day. Part of the preparation for the wedding was to have their hands traditionally painted with henna designs, still visible after several days of wear and washing. Beautiful. Just hearing them talk about the wedding weekend with so much enjoyment, smiles, and laughter helped me let go of some of the annoyances with their country's controls I continued to carry.

Those conversations were my window into their lives. I never got the impression they felt like second-class citizens: having to walk behind their men, not being allowed to drive, or have a job. They were the holders of the family purse strings; they made decisions about their home, food, cars, clothing, children, and travel which must have been a considerable responsibility for Aminah's mother and aunty. In a country where women were not permitted to work, managing that financial load must have represented a responsibility, but could it also have felt like a source of power to them?

We kept in touch after I returned to England in 1983, and when they brought Aminah to London, I was always invited to meet them for a meal, like old friends, even though we never used first names when addressing each other.

Getting to know and work with Aminah one hour a week wasn't quite enough to overcome feelings of isolation as I stayed in the flat, day after day, even with sewing, letter writing, and an occasional bus ride into town to keep me busy. I needed more work, and I had an idea where to find it.

Every time I rode the bus into Jeddah, I noticed a small sign in Arabic and English with an arrow pointing to Baksh Hospital. The time had come to investigate. It was a short walk from a bus stop around a corner to the large modern, three-story building with a couple of taxis waiting close to the curb. The familiar antiseptic smell of hospital greeted me as I entered the swinging front doors into a wide, white reception area full of people on the move. Joining them was easy. Appropriately dressed, I just merged with the walkers, past the closed doors of the Physiotherapy Department, getting a feel for adjacent offices identified by signs in both languages, one of which was: Personnel Department. Bingo!

The sunny room was furnished with expensive-looking wooden desks, the latest style of office chairs and pinkish horizontal metal file cabinets, something I'd never seen before. There were five or six young men busy on their telephones or typewriters. Realizing I had arrived with little forethought for what I was about to do, I jumped when a bearded, young man in a crisp white *thobe* suddenly appeared and asked if I had an appointment? Could he help me? Well, 'No,' and 'Yes, he could.' Too late, as I started to explain that I was interested in employment as an Occupational Therapist, ooops I was on the brink of breaking the law again: no work visa. But the young man was all smiles, 'Yes, you are welcome,' he spoke in English. I relaxed a little. Not only had the subject of a visa not come up, but I hadn't brought a copy of my Canadian OT registration and license with me, in spite of which, I was invited to join him at a table for an interview. Within an hour, I walked out of that serene room with a job: part-time physiotherapist, four hours a day for three days, a twelve-hour week. Perfect. And the hospital was on a bus route.

Smug and smiling, I climbed into the empty back of the bus for the ride home: I had another job.

My university education in *Montréal* was a combined Occupational/Physical Therapy course. All students took pre-med classes somewhere, then came together for a year of exposure to the theory and modalities of both types of therapy. After which, I chose to concentrate on occupational therapy, but having that basic understanding of physiotherapy principles proved to be extraordinarily useful throughout my career, particularly in this instance.

Baksh Hospital's phisiotherapy department was small, an out-patient facility for male patients only, with the majority of treatments taking place in patient's private rooms on the upper floors. On the first morning, I was introduced to the therapists, familiarized with the department and hospital, then had my questions answered, specifically the one about: how to handle conversations with men, according to Saudi law. The answers reflected what I'd hoped to hear: within the department, eye contact, conversation, and some touches were protected by therapeutic protocol. Hearing that was an enormous relief.

My responsibilities were to assist two certified physiotherapists, a Swedish lady and a South African man, by taking on some of the more routine procedures thereby freeing them to address specific treatments beyond my knowledge. My initial focus was the very basic, nothing fancy, traction machine.

There must have been plenty of legitimate referrals, but why were there so many Saudi men with terrible back trouble? The therapist in me wondered if some patients, themselves controlled by the rule forbidding them to talk with or be seen with an unrelated woman, had discovered how to do both, legally. If so, the Swedish therapist and I both became 'that woman'. Could my assumption be correct: that some had feigned a severe back problem for which their doctor prescribed physiotherapy? After my experience with the purple penis, I had suspicions.

Grateful to my lady friends on the bus, I could use polite greetings with my patients, always *'Marhaba, Kayf halik?'* ('Hello, how are you?'), and the usual reply, *'elHamdilla, shukran'* ('Fine, thanks'). Once the patient was connected to traction, communication was by grunts, gestures, smiles, frowns, and body language, unless they spoke English. It worked.

The machine was set up in an open space; my job was to position the patient on a special table, attach a belt around the hips, place a pillow under the knees, add an appropriate amount of weight to create traction, and set a timer. No matter how carefully I performed those movements there were times when I touched the patient for which I quickly apologized. I chose to follow up with hot packs to a patient's back, allowing the treatment to be done through clothing. To teach good body mechanics for standing, bending, reaching, and picking up objects from the floor, I decided to move myself and have the patient imitate me. My treatments became fun. Slowly I was finding a balance between being able to shed the apprehension that I would accidentally break the law and be in trouble, and confidence that I wouldn't. Having never worked as a physiotherapist before, this was a congenial and safe place to practice and learn; my patients loved the attention, and I enjoyed a perverse feeling of power.

It's probably a universal tradition for patients to give a token of appreciation to caregivers when their treatment is over. Our Saudi patients were no different. Frequently fresh flowers flown to Jeddah from Holland or England, and fine imported Belgium chocolates would appear on the reception desk with a note of thanks. These we all shared, though neither flowers nor chocolates made the trip home intact, not in the intense midday heat on the bus. Occasionally a small gift-box was given to one of us individually in which would be a gift of gold. I once received a delicate necklace with my name in Arabic letters and on another occasion, a little finger ring that held a ruby, how lovely.

Once when I was in a hurry to visit a patient on an upper floor, my way was blocked by two very large men in traditional *thobes* deep in conversation. They occupied the center of the hallway, taking up most of its width, narrowing the space on either side of them where people were hurrying by. Realizing that space between them was wide enough for me to slip through, I excused myself, bent my knees to be less conspicuous and quickly passed between them. From my colleagues, I later learned that the taller, larger of the two was Idi Amin, and the other as Dr. Baksh himself. Idi Amin, who once was the brutally cruel President of Uganda, lived exiled in Jeddah until his death in 2003. He might have been a patient of Dr. Baksh. Under different circumstances and during a different time in history, I could have been eliminated for my risky maneuver. What luck to have safely managed it. I took a big breath of gratitude and a moment to recall the calming memory of Rouen Cathedral's rose window.

Looking back on these experiences with Saudi people, I realized there was a similarity between my-not-so-well-off Saudi bus mates, the family with plenty of money, and the large variety of men who passed through the physiotherapy department. They gave me the impression their wealth or status wasn't overly important to any of them. They all seemed to accept their lot. I regret that the two elderly Yemeni gate guards at 16 House Compound who were not Saudi, and my bus mates who were, I knew only superficially. Whereas Aminah's family, who were Saudi, whose first names I wasn't invited to use, remained acquaintances. Even though I was entertained by them, I felt I was an employee. Their invitation to join them in London might have been a pleasant formality, I'll never know. Now I regret not being on friendly terms with any Saudis.

What impressed me most, was what I learned later from the English newspapers about the deep supportive relationships between women across the Saudi social spectrum: the brave activists who fought for years for permission to drive cars, and be allowed to vote. My own observations illustrated the obvious friendships between the ladies in the back of the bus and Amina's mother and aunty who tirelessly supported their child while living surrounded by incredible wealth. From that small sample of experiences, the lessons and lasting impressions they taught me were that Saudi people were loyal to the historic, desert dwellers traditions of hospitality and generosity. Whatever they had to share they willingly did. Practices Terry and I incorporated into our lifestyle.

The government was something else.

27

Not Again

I had no choice.

I'd stayed too late at the hospital and missed the bus. The fifty-minute walk alone to Saudia City would not only put me at considerable risk but was impossible since I needed to be home before Roger returned from school. Without a grandmotherly sort of person I could go to for advice, this was a dilemma I'd foreseen and feared because it meant having to chance taking a taxi alone. There was no real reason to be fearful. I hadn't heard any frightening stories from friends since none of them had ever taken a taxi alone, it was just the recent accumulation of strange experiences, so full of unpleasant potential, that filled me with dread.

There was only one taxi waiting outside the hospital's front door. I made my way to it through a flock of people and approached with a look and gesture that asked the driver if he was available. He gave a nod. I took a deep breath, climbed into the back seat on the passenger side, repositioned my head scarf, hugged my small backpack on my lap and, in my best Arabic, gave the driver my Saudia

City, East Gate destination. Soon familiar landmarks of art on the *Corniche* and pristine beaches flashed by. Occasionally, in my peripheral vision, I noticed the driver, an older, grey-haired man, staring at me in the rear-view mirror. What was he thinking?

A right turn off the dual carriageway and then another quick right turn would have put the car on the loop road around a large, almost empty lot on the south side of Saudia City. It was about the size of a football field, owned by a lesser prince who had constructed his palace compound on a far corner with more palaces planned as his family and prestige grew. But instead of making any turn, the taxi driver pointed his vehicle straight into the emptiness on a deeply rutted track I had never noticed. An alarm went off in my head. Clutching my backpack close to my body, I prepared my thoughts in anticipation of the next surprise. Dodging pieces of broken concrete and other large, abandoned construction debris, the driver navigated obstacles pulling the steering wheel left and right.

In what seemed to be the center of the vast space, the vehicle came to an abrupt stop. It was very quiet. The wrinkled old man stiffly turned to me, his look triumphant and, casually putting his arm on the back of his seat, settled himself for a friendly little chat. Not with me. That was my cue. Without hesitation and taking careful aim, I swung my pack at him, which was awkward in such a confined space, and hit his arm and shoulder, giving me time to open the door and jump out, grateful again for morning exercise in the parking lot at 16 House Compound.

My long skirt immediately tried to trip me as I started to make an earnest dash for the distant East Gate, my *abâya* billowing out behind me. I didn't look back, but knew he must have watched my progress, perhaps in disbelief. Those potholes and construction obstacles continued to litter the track, some I had to jump over. Not easy as my backpack strap kept slipping off my shoulder, my headscarf threatened to throttle me and my skirt insisted on bunching up between my legs, slowing my pace. Determined to outsmart the old man, I ran with feelings of fury and disdain until I safely arrived at my destination, a little winded and very relieved that I was home before Roger. With a quick glance over my shoulder, I saw the taxi was gone.

He didn't get paid.

———

Being kidnapped and taken to the empty center of a huge, abandoned construction site was enough to discourage me from any future solo taxi rides in Jeddah. So, I could never miss the bus again. The distance between 16 House Compound and Saudia City took a manageable thirty-five minutes and I had discovered two possible routes. The most expeditious was along the sidewalk of the busy main north-bound road, but exposure and fumes increased my vulnerability. The other, less direct route through a hodge-podge of residential side streets, took a little longer but was easier walking. The route I chose depended on my need to hurry home. If Roger wasn't with me, I'd be listening to Bee Gees or Moody Blues music through headphones from the Walkman in my pocket, my rhythmical stride and upright posture announcing, 'Don't even think about messing with me.' But some Saudi men, seemingly unable to heed my body language, tried annoying ways to trip me up.

While walking north along the sidewalk next to traffic, the constant drone of speeding cars felt protective, I was safe as long as cars continued to fly past. Until the day I became aware of a ponderously slow vehicle moving closely behind me. Had it slowed to turn into one of the driveways punctuating the sidewalk? I increased my speed, but so did the car.

That triggered an old memory of fear and confusion from an incident that happened in Marrakesh, Morocco, during the summer Minitrek Expedition, in 1960. Our travels had taken us from London through France and Spain to Morocco. After a solo afternoon exploration of Djema el Fna, Marrakesh's huge main square with its snake charmers and water vendors, I waved to my friends and was about to cross the road to meet them in a *café*, when unexpectedly, a car stopped beside me. Its back passenger door flew open, hands reached from inside, grabbed my left arm and pulled hard to unbalance me. At the same time someone was pulling on my right arm shaking and twisting, determined to release the hold of the person in the car. Was this a bad dream, this rag doll like feeling of being torn apart by opposing forces? I used all my effort to resist being pulled closer to the car's back seat.

Then I was free. The door slammed shut, screeching tires and angry Arabic shouting faded into the humid air.

The person pulling on my right arm let go too, then caught me as, disoriented and unsupported, I lost my balance. My friends, who moments before had returned my wave, also noticed that something was amiss, ran to me concerned and thanked the young man who had come to my rescue. They wanted to know what had happened. To get the whole story, we made our way to the coffee shop terrace where my rescuer told us about the many white-slave kidnappings taking place in Marrakesh. He had recognized the *modus operandi* and had rushed to help me. A true hero.

I was reminded of that experience as the car in Jeddah matched my speed just behind me. I didn't dare look, but was there someone in the back seat waiting to grab me? I surveyed my surroundings. Homes along that stretch of road were like armed forts with high walls and solid metal gates protecting their entrances, often with a turreted gate house that had two doors, one with street access and another opening into the garden. With no time to hesitate, a sudden flash of inspiration gave me the idea to trust a nearby gate house as a possible opportunity for escape. The temptation was irresistible. I walked confidently up to the door and tried the knob, it turned. I entered nonchalantly, closing the door behind me. What luck and what a great discovery.

Though obviously trespassing, I remained there only long enough to assure myself that my suspected assailant had accelerated and was merging into north bound traffic. Then, I confidently stepped onto the sidewalk and continued to make my way home without incident, relieved and amused that the Bee Gee's song 'Stayin' Alive' filled my ears. It was an audacious but necessary behaviour I never had to use again, but I was prepared.

Back in Marrakesh, my rescuer introduced himself as Benatia Aomar and, as if he hadn't already done enough by saving my life, his mother invited my travel buddies and me, all seven of us, to their home the following afternoon for a traditional Moroccan meal. With easy English,

French and some Arabic bantering, we sat at a long table on an upper balcony looking out over a lovely garden, walled with cobalt blue and white tiles; gurgling fountains, bright pink bougainvillea, and a profusion of jasmine climbing all around us, its perfume filling the air. Benatia's mother brought out a large tajin of tender lamb and vegetables, taught us how to eat using only the fingers of our right hand. It was one of those amazing evenings which brings complete strangers together to share and respect our unique and common humanity. It was a day and a night to relish and remember with gratitude.

Benatia and I, both at universities, both enjoying the same music, exchanged letters in English for many years until the thread of our friendship finally frayed. But I've never forgotten the terror of being pulled back and forth, or his quick response that saved my life, his family's kindness and the long friendship we shared.

28

Friday's Freedom

Friday, the Muslim holy day, a lovely morning in September 1982. We were back in our fourth floor flat in Saudia City and this was my time to do what I loved most.

———

Out of the apartment and down the marble staircase that spirals around the elevator shaft I race, clickety click, as my shoes take step after quick step. Then across the stone-clad entrance hall and out, out into the heat and humidity that hits me like a body blow, out into another calm and quiet Friday morning in Jeddah. I've left Roger still asleep and Terry making coffee, I'll have a cup at my destination in the city.

Carefully dressed so as not to draw attention: my flowery cotton skirt is long enough to cover my ankles, white silky sleeves long enough to cover my wrists, and collar high enough to cover my neck. The bus driver is revving the engine impatiently so I must hurry along the empty, sandy road and through the Saudia City East Gate. But when I pick up my long skirt to run it bunches up between my legs, my black silk *abâya* billows out behind like the Flying Nun's and the black silk scarf over my hair threatens to fall off. These Saudi guardianship rules are not made for runners.

Once again, I'm the only passenger in the women's section at the back of the bus. Leaning onto the already hot and sticky, black plastic bench, I close my eyes in anticipation of this day's adventure.

If I take a camera, caution is necessary to surreptitiously use it as the driver slowly negotiates narrow roads. We are approaching the old city, I'm a sea bird, able to cruise the streets just feet off the ground. I poke my nose into hidden corners; up tiny shady lanes, over garden walls, into beautifully tiled, flower-filled spaces and empty restaurant grounds, closed and dark coffee shops, past snugly parked cars.

Close to town old buildings take on height and stature, four, five, even six stories of elegance, their swaths of wooden additions that, with a closer look are balconies, loggias, and bay windows, intricately patterned and cleverly designed to serve double duty: to allow women and girls to privately look out onto the street and to allow cool mountain breezes from the east and refreshing offshore gusts to circulate throughout the rooms. Even today those high balconies have no glass covering their windows.

Friday's Freedom

Greetings Oh you seated in the latticed balcony
And exalted high above all the people[1]

I love their ornate fretwork and verandas, the wood aged and dulled by the passage of time and winds from the sea carrying salty humidity which gives them a velvety, grey finish. Although it is illegal, I just can't resist photographing them until my camera becomes a burden I leave at home.

Although many have been allowed to deteriorate, there are now over one thousand traditional Islamic buildings near the old suq, of which over five hundred are listed as having extraordinary architectural and historic significance. This designation protects and preserves the essence of the old structures, as glass, steel, and concrete are introduced.

The route is familiar, so my choice of where to alight is decided by a mood or a conversation I've had with friends, something old or something new to explore. To see every one of those listed homes is my goal.

A short walk and I pass the only large department store, it's wide windows hold no interest for me this morning. Rather I take a cobbled path into the once walled suq and

---

1 Jeddah Old and New, page 53. Published by: Stacey International, London.

find myself following a narrow passage lined with tiny shops. Behind their glass fronted, brightly lit windows and doors gleam breathtaking, glistening beauty... Gold! The shops are small. Many jammed close together, often selling the same pieces of jewelry: yards of chain necklaces, some resembling gold armour, trays of jeweled rings and ruby-red, velvet-covered rods on which hang a profusion of earrings. By standing with my forehead against a glass door I let my eyes travel around the dazzling displays, up and down in slow concentration, leaving a nose print as a memento. A shop selling international brands of gold watches for women and men catches my attention. I might treat myself to a small Omega with the money I make at the hospital.

It's so quiet, the town could be asleep.

Then, as I approach the local mosque, a loud tinny voice reverberates from speakers atop its tall white minaret, its message infiltrates every corner. My pace slows, there's a rustling, muted sounds of activity and I begin to cross paths with local folk on their way to answer the prayer call. It's surprising to see how many people actually live squirreled away behind their tiny shops. I whisper 'Marhaba' as I walk past those patiently leaning against a wall of the mosque, waiting to wash their feet in the little fountain embedded in the stones near two or three much worn steps, each already covered with dusty, well-used shoes and sandals. How does all that footwear later manage to find the feet that had walked them there, so many of them look the same?

Soon the narrow path empties and sounds waft from the mosque's open front doors. What does the inside look like and what's going on in there? I'm not curious enough to join the black-clad women as they pass through their special entrance, although I suppose I could. Dressed exactly like them, the only difference between us is invisible.

———

From earlier travels, I have memories of colourful Spanish and Moroccan mosques with cobalt blue, white, orange tiled walls, ceilings, and floors, circular rippling fountains and quotes from the Quran intricately carved in stone. Visitors are invited to enter and appreciate their historic beauty. But as guardian of the Sunni sect, Saudi Arabia welcomes no infidels into their mosques. Even the holy cities of Mecca and Medina are hidden behind mountains, though we have spied them briefly from the bypass road.

Acknowledging the mystery, I allow myself to be drawn deeper into the suq tempted by lingering ancient aromas of closed spice shops, just looking to explore some newly discovered row of workers' small homes with classic arched doorways. Behind them rise those historic relics, with their asymmetry and precariously cantilevered balconies that shade the narrow passage below, creating a canyon for me to walk through. T.E. Lawrence aptly described these lanes as 'alleys, narrow for shade,' they haven't changed. These very old buildings of coralline limestone blocks taken from the sea, now eroded and blackened, are tall proud homes still lived in. I could spend the morning examining their original old wooden doors, perhaps made of imported mahogany, each with its intricately carved story from the Quran.

To experience this uniquely Islamic city center is both a comfort and a quest. Without books, newspapers, or museums and with only a rudimentary knowledge of Arabic, it is difficult for me to find understanding and answers, especially to the question: are all the guardianship rules actually from the Quran? But I can walk and see and smell and listen. The walks are therapy. The defiance they require allows me to protest controls I so dislike. They replenish my spirit and strengthen my resolve to be as independent as possible in spite of the laws and to open a space in my days for acceptance.

After getting my fill of solitude, I know I can't linger, the bus won't wait. So I am content to wander over and stand at the kiosk by the bus stop for my tiny cup of smoking hot cardamom coffee before taking a seat in the back for the ride home.

As the driver navigates the way northward, my thoughts drift to my visit in the calm, empty heart of the old town, giving me time to ponder contrasts. Contrasts between my familiar world and this one: between our cultures, languages, church bells and prayer calls, commercial traditions, clothing, attitudes toward women, and to notice the differences between this day's quietness and the crazy hustle-bustle, noise, crowds, and fumes of weekdays. I appreciate the challenges old Jeddah faces with the new world irritatingly rubbing up against its shoulders.

A familiar right turn off the *Corniche*. I could see the East Gate terminus across the huge empty lot I once traversed in panic, a recollection that no longer haunted me. It was time to correctly present myself: *abâya* clutched tightly around my body and my *hijab* repositioned to hide my hair. I was ready to climb down those steep steps and leave the bus. As always, I gave the driver a generous 'Thank You' wave since in effect he had been my private chauffeur, and calmly headed through the East Gate for home. As I climbed the stairs that hugged the elevators, I noticed my steps were more deliberate, slow and strong. I felt grounded, knowing I was ready to return to family responsibilities, secure in the memories I'd created by the morning's saunters along Jeddah's Friday streets.

29

Wrong Side of the Law

I was putting Roger to bed with a story when I heard my name shouted outside. From the road. One quick frantic syllable, then silence.

Cautiously looking down over the large, crude concrete window box that hugged the living room wall, I saw a Saudia City police car coming to a stop at the entrance to our building. Within seconds our front door was flung open, and Terry almost fell inside the flat spluttering as he tried to catch his breath. He closed the door and carefully locked it. He'd run up the stairs, to the fourth floor.

If Terry believed the police had chased him as far as the building, he must have suspected their reason: something related to fermenting grapes? In spite of regulations which forbade this practice, our vino tinto from fruit juice and sugar was pretty good. There was always lots for our own enjoyment and for many friends we regularly entertained. The contents of five illegal sweet-smelling buckets percolated with musical bubbles and froth in the back corners of my large kitchen pantry. Terry wasn't the most athletic man, but scared enough, he mustered the energy to run upstairs without leaving a tell-tale message on the elevator indicator to show the police which floor to check first.

We needed to get to work. I opened the pantry door and turned to see Terry's frantic gesticulations. Hurry! So I slid the heavy buckets with their precious sloshing brew across the kitchen floor into the living room where Terry had precariously stationed himself in the deep, empty window box. My few potted herbs were quickly put aside. One by one, I pushed the buckets over to the window, one by one, Terry lifted them over the sill then slid them to the dark corner where they were completely hidden. His plan: to stash them there, out of sight of the morality police when they made their appearance which he instinctively knew they would do.

In spite of the panic, we got the job done, all the buckets were safe. I wiped up a few splashes on the kitchen and living room floors. But had he been detected up there, standing in the window box?

'This is crazy, can we get away with it?' I whispered in the dark. I couldn't help wondering if this hobby was worth the fear that had just consumed him and infected me too. 'We have no choice, and you know it.' he hissed, as he climbed back into the living room and closed the window.

I knew he was right. We had to protect our secret. We knew the risk and the consequences because the news had spread quickly throughout the expatriate community on the morning of Eddie's arrest. We couldn't believe it. No one knew until then, that secreted in his back bedroom was a very sophisticated still making *sidiki* 'my friend,' illegal spirits similar in clarity and taste to vodka. Illegal in Jeddah, but much in demand.

Eddie and Elizabeth were our good friends. Of their five children, their eldest son, Jeremy, was Roger's buddy at school. It was a hint of a smell that had given our friend away to a neighbour who thought he detected the aroma of beer in the air as he walked on the path behind Eddie's home. Making beer would have been a minor transgression. Once inside the home, the morality police found the *sidiki* still and Eddie was removed.

In Jeddah, prison was intended to be, by its reputation, a deterrent to breaking the law. We started to hear ugly stories of Saudi jails, their overcrowding and lack of food, and the frequent misplacement of paperwork that kept men languishing long after their sentences were completed. Without family support, prisoners could starve to death. We knew the terrible reality of Eddie's situation because I often helped Elizabeth by taking meals to him. When I caught sight of his white face I'd give him time to battle his way to the front of the crowd then pass the lunch package through a wall of steel bars where men, begging for food and attention, were lined up. Dozens of hairy, white-knuckled men held on, determined to keep their position as those behind juggled for a place in the front. The smell and angry shouting really disturbed me. Hunger and frustration expressed on prisoners' faces told a dehumanizing story. Dreadful both for the suffering human beings hanging onto that metal grill and for our friends who were separated by it. They had known the consequences of the risks they had taken. So did we.

⌒

I lit a vanilla scented candle to hide any sweet, musty smells that lingered and by the time the police *did* knock on our door we were at the table in the candle's soft glow. We hoped we looked relaxed, our untouched supper before us. We both wore pretend smiles and oozed innocent regret for the inconvenience someone had caused our uniformed visitors. They didn't recognize Terry and they didn't take us up on the invitation to look around. We were so bold. They apologized and headed to the door eager to continue their mission. Terry saw them out. After he closed the front door and locked it behind them, he fell against it in relief. Slumped in our chairs, we relaxed with a glass of wine and congratulated each other on our brazened coolness, bemused but utterly shaken by what might have happened. A strange bittersweet feeling of success tinged with guilt filled my thoughts, guilt that had made us both assume the morality police were looking for evidence of illicit alcohol making. I didn't regret the frantic action we had taken to be safe.

Unable to actually eat the supper I'd made and with muted voices so as not to disturb our sleeping son, we continued to discuss why and what had happened. Did the discovery of Eddie's illegal still increase police vigilance in Saudia City? Were other apartment blocks targeted? Could a smell have alerted one of our neighbours? Suppose after those first few successful batches of wine we had become *blasé*, relaxed in conversations and behaviour, and forgotten to protect our secret. Perhaps Terry had been noticed at Leb Joe's grocery store frequently buying large amounts of sugar and grape juice. Possibly a neighbour was suspicious of all the entertaining we did, since three or four times a week we were joined by several of Terry's noisy port-employee friends, who loved a glass or two of wine with their supper.

I knew there were police whose job it was to monitor what we expatriates were doing, especially when it came to alcohol. Yet, in spite of this potential danger, many of us nurtured our little kitchen wineries. Terry and I successfully continued to for the four years we lived there. We were motivated by both the challenge of making wine in a completely dry country and of enjoying a glass when we wanted one. We weren't alone in that endeavour.

We had friends who never made wine or even drank it during their time in the Kingdom. Because they chose to obey the laws, they never experienced a similar episode of trepidation and obvious guilt. We rationalized that the rules we broke were based on Islamic religious principles. They were not our principles. By breaking the 'no alcohol' rule for our own consumption, in our own home, there was no Saudi involvement. Perhaps Eddie's[1] *sidiki*, which he sold, might have reached Saudi hands and that would definitely have been a serious infraction of the morality law.

The panic we'd experienced from the threat of discovery didn't change the way we ultimately thought about the risks we continued to take. Instead, living in defiance provided a sense of freedom, independence, and even excitement. It was one of the ways we found to endure living there, in spite of the rules.

If I asked, I was never told just what it was that put such a scare into Terry that night, it remained his secret.

Cheers!

---

1 Eddie's imprisonment lasted two years. Upon his release and return to Ireland, Roger and I paid them a celebratory visit.

30

Agents of Change

The longer Roger and I stayed in Jeddah the more we discovered opportunities for exploration with our American friends. Since Roger and Paul were such good buddies, our families would join forces, and if there was an empty seat or two in a vehicle, there was always someone happy to join us, a classmate of Rogers or neighbours from the American compounds.

———

We accepted many invitations from our geologist friends and once drove with them in their Land Rover east across the desert along old camel trails, zigging and zagging towards the road up the escarpment to deliciously cool Taif, at 5,500 feet elevation on the plateau. There we set up tents in an open, sandy depression around a fire pit, chairs scattered about providing us views of boulders piled high enough for me to climb up and scramble over, an activity I'd enjoyed since childhood. Many boulders scattered haphazardly on the ground invited the boys to climb, for us all to play hide and seek. Friendly fun and precious freedom. Sitting outside in the early morning coolness with a cup of coffee, the smell of potatoes sizzling in butter nearby, was like a dream come true. There were bugs in the high country too, one large clumsy black flying insect amused us when it dove at terrific speed into a steaming coffee mug. The splash made us all jump.

An alternative curvy route down to sea level provided opportunities to make stops at village bazaars where I haggled over the prices of used Bedouin treasures. First, I spied a heavy bracelet encrusted with thick black dirt. At the next village, an old tent divider of faded red, orange, purple rough woven wool called to me. Further on, at a small stall on the roadside near a tented home, a collection of garments were piled haphazardly on a rickety table. There, in the jumble of well-worn clothes, I found a rustic home-made black and aqua cotton dress with hundreds of meticulously handmade, tiny silver or tin decorations. I still have them all. The heavy bracelet, after it spent a night soaking in Coca Cola, became a solid silver, wearable piece of art, cleverly carved with a simple, decorated closure. Roger wears it now. The tent divider, used in long Bedouin tents to separate a family's men and women, makes a novel carpet for our little old house in France, and the no-longer-smelly dress still adorns my living room wall for all to admire the intricate decorations that make it so unique.

To the north, beyond Saudia City was 'the creek', a name given to a curve in the coast, hugging a sandy beach and a somewhat protected expanse of sea. We were fortunate enough to occasionally borrow a seaside property there from a friend who rented it. It met our basic needs with its wobbly, creaky wooden hut for shade and privacy, and a long wharf projecting away from the shore. This was really important because between the beach and deep water lurked stonefish (Synanceia), the most potent poisonous fish on the planet! Coincidentally, in Nigeria, I'd been visited by that country's most venomous snake (Dendroapsis *viridis*). I survived both encounters. In spite of their excellent camouflage, by lying very still on the wharf on my belly, and peering studiously into the murky water, I could spy stonefish resting on the bottom, rolling slowly from side to side by gentle wave action. From the end of the wharf, Roger, Paul and friends could safely spend all afternoon, diving, jumping, and playing in deep water with loud delighted shouts, knowing never to touch bottom. This little slice of sandy shore gave us so much forbidden pleasure, relaxing there in comfort, in bathing suits, unseen by curious Saudis. We could picnic, take friends, and pretend we were somewhere else.

On the way home, with tired, salty children asleep in the back seat, we would slowly drive past the new enormous and handsome Hajj Airport Terminal with its vast white tent-inspired roof line. Since Jeddah is the port of entry for hundreds of thousands of Hajj attendees coming from every corner of the world for the annual pilgrimage to the holiest city of Mecca, this airport had been built exclusively to accommodate them. During some years, as many as a million visitors were counted, all arriving within a few days. Its interior would have to be cavernous. How I wanted to see it. But like Jeddah's mosques, the inside of this intriguing building had to remain a mystery to me, an infidel. Hoping for a glimpse through an open door, I had to be content with admiring it from the car as we cruised by after every visit to the creek.

With money I earned over those three and a half years in Jeddah, I'd promised myself a visit to the international watch shop where, on that first visit to the suq, I spied a gold Omega with a tiny diamond on its face. Years later, when I was ready to make a purchase, the shop's proprietor offered to size it since it flopped about on my thin wrist, and I agreed. When I collected my pretty new watch and tried it on, the fit was perfect, but where was the piece of gold band that had been cut off (about 4cms) which I had bought and considered it mine to reuse somehow. Without speaking English or French, the shop keeper shrugged his shoulders and shook his head 'Sorry.' I knew I'd been outsmarted. But it was OK.

Red Sea beaches were a diver's delight before hundreds of Filipino men, brought into the Kingdom to do menial work during our second year in Jeddah, quickly did what they were used to doing at home: fishing for their breakfast, lunch, and supper in the waters close to their homes in the city. To avoid them, we had the luxury of traveling both north and south to explore beaches with intact, beautiful, unblemished reefs. One special beach we discovered several miles north of the desalination plant became a favourite. As we waded through shallow water for about ten minutes before donning our flippers and tanks and descending over the reef, a small octopus frequently befriended us, suddenly appearing near someone's toes, dazzling us with its flashing colours, then scooting away like a tiny torpedo into deep water. It obviously recognized the rhythmic sounds coming from three or four sets of splashing feet and came to say 'Hello!' Was it the wonders of that stretch of reef or the friendship of that little fella that called us back to dive there?

To the north and south, there were miles of easy access to deep pristine water, where a sheer cliff of coral teamed with rich aquatic abundance including occasional large species. I often had to hold my breath and stay as still as if I were a statue, as sharks cruised by me and flotillas of sleek silvery barracuda paraded in formation above, hoping they were more interested in smaller prey than me. In these clear and clean waters, with encouragement from my coach, I was proud to fulfill my goal of becoming a DiveMaster scuba diver, completing all the requirements including a free ascent from ninety feet, an exhilarating achievement. Sadly, during the three and a half years I swam along the reef, its plenitude of fish and plant life became noticeably diminished.

Including my successful Friday walks alone in the suq, all those adventures helped me become a different person: busy, happy, confident. Over time I discovered I'd matured, no longer beating my head against the Saudi rules I had initially found so humiliating.

Many expatriate friends never set foot outside the compound they were assigned to, many never ventured out on public buses which were both safe and free. I wonder what kind of impression Saudi Arabia, Jeddah in particular, might have made on them. How would they describe the time they spent there? As a hardship? Our lives were enriched because I was determined to experience whatever I could. We were fortunate to have befriended people who had freedom to travel beyond the confines of their homes. They facilitated my attitude shift: from rejection of Saudi rules to accepting what the country had to offer.

31

Clearing the Path

'Not all storms come to disrupt your life.
Some come to clear your path.'
~*Paulo Coelho*

In late autumn of 1982, a low cloud darkened the sky. It brought an artificial dusk as it hung over Jeddah, dumping its gift on a dry, hot desert, its drops huge enough to form divots in the sandy Saudia City roads, turning them to muddy tracks. We watched, transfixed, having never experienced such meteorological violence in this city. During our time in Jeddah there had been trifling rains and mischievous winds, nothing like this. It wasn't quite a hurricane, but it was powerful and exhilarating.

I reflected how, as a new 'arrivee' back in mid-1979, my life in Jeddah had been a storm of unexpected experiences that filled me with anger and despair. I had felt belittled, my independence challenged and my true identity subdued. Initially I wasn't prepared to sit back and accept the Saudi rules and regulations, in fact, they seemed to empower my defiance.

The winds of that fierce thunderstorm uprooted trees, blew out windows. Its rains caused extensive road erosion. Lives were lost when vehicles were driven or fell into vast, water-filled cavities. Everyone seemed to have a story.

Roger and I saw a VW Beetle nosedive into a huge pothole between 16 and 8 House Compounds, only its shiny back bumper visible above the muddy water. Its occupants managing to quickly escape. Driving with Terry, I saw what happened when, in spite of a large warning sign in both languages saying: CAUTION: LARGE 4 METER PUDDLE the driver and passenger of a Cadillac, only the tips of its white fins visible above the murky brown surface, might not have been so lucky when it almost disappeared outside the American Embassy. And from his balcony in 16 House Compound, our friend George watched as the driver of a convertible Volkswagen drove across the busy intersection just as a manhole cover suddenly flew into the air, propelled by massive gushes of water, geyser like, which escaped from an overloaded storm drain under the road. One of the car's front wheels fell into the hole, suddenly trapping the car under a shower of filthy water as the driver successfully ran away.

There were many such stories.

———

Within days after that storm, with potholes in the roads still full of water, we moved into a brand-new marble-clad flat just two blocks east of 16 House Compound. It was an upgrade in accommodation, part of a package Terry received when he was promoted to an elite Special Flights crew flying Gulf Stream jets carrying VIPs including Yassar Arafat and members of the Saudi Royal family. I shouldn't have been surprised, but it did disappoint me to notice that in my spacious, mirrored bathroom, a bidet was just placed on the tiled floor, not plumbed into the system. It just sat there.

While roads were still full of puddles, Roger and I had our own quick brush with calamity. On our way to our fabulous new flat, we stood together at a corner, waiting to cross a road pockmarked with all sizes of potholes, looking like modern art; their muddy surfaces reflected a still grey sky. The curb where we stood marked the edge of a large puddle almost two meters long, rippling against the curb, threatening to spill over onto the sidewalk.

As we chatted, I noticed a car accelerating towards us, a couple of kids in the front seats, the driver's look intense. Anticipating being drenched, 'Quickly Roger, step back!' As we did, the car abruptly stopped in front of us with a loud clunk and took on a serious lean in our direction. Two occupants flopped forwards and back like puppets, grins wiped off their faces. Immediately the driver threw open his door, leapt out, hands on hips, big eyed in disbelief. He stomped around to the front of his vehicle while cursing us in loud, angry Arabic. What had we done?

His passenger couldn't move. His feet were probably getting wet; at least a third of his door was under water, jammed against the curb, the front wheel hidden in the dirty puddle. While the driver's open door was an invitation to escape, it was also an uphill climb that seemed to overwhelm the passenger. With his *keffiyah* askew, he hung his head out of the window giving us killer stares. Their behaviour was so fascinating to watch. The driver seemed enraged. He kept hopping about bellowing with frustration, beating a fist in the air. He bounced into the car, tried to start the engine. When it failed to respond, he jumped out, slammed the door, this time splashing around behind the car to the dry sidewalk where we gave him plenty of space and watched as he knelt to examine the problem, his *thobe* all wet and clinging to his skinny legs. His pathetic companion still trapped in his seat, ignored. The driver, realizing their little game had backfired; his car wasn't going anywhere, gave the rear tyre a powerful kick with his sandaled foot. Ouch.

Prompted by memories of those many unpleasant experiences I had suffered when, with my independent attitude, I was being introduced to the realities of life in Jeddah, my vindictive thought was, *'serves you right.'*

In the early days of 1983, as Roger's eighth birthday was approaching, Terry, in one of his 'Oh, by the way' moments, confessed to having signed-up Roger, when he was a baby, to attend an expensive English boy's school called Eagle House in Surrey, about forty miles west of London. We would have to enroll him immediately after his birthday in early March. Terry assured me he had found a reliable, unnamed friend to watch over our son in our absence since he had decided I'd be staying in Jeddah. Both ideas—Roger attending a private school as a boarder with someone I didn't know checking on him—and me remaining in Jeddah without Roger—were choices I completely rejected.

Although the big promotion to Special Flights must have provided wonderful experiences for Terry, they actually were the brunt of a wedge that slammed into our family life by taking him away from home for weeks at a time, without us knowing where he was. He could have been anywhere and often was, as I discovered, when photos of unknown people and places showed up in his suit case; black silk undies and two mismatched earrings also. My knees collapsed and I sank to the floor to pick them up. His message was clear. For months I had known the gulf between us was widening and now I had to confront it.

During a subsequent very short conversation when I expressed my curiosity and frustrations, Terry's response was: 'admit it Joan, you've had a pretty good life under me' which was absolutely true, as these stories describe. But 'under him?' He wouldn't explain. Was he so angered by my unwavering independence and determination to make my own decisions that he felt pushed away?

Still in early March 1983, Terry's flying contract with Saudia Airlines suddenly ended.

That wild storm, having created such havoc in Jeddah, blew similar chaotic changes, and the solution, into our lives: it was time for the three of us to make an exit from the Kingdom of Saudi Arabia.

We took a couple of days to pack up another home. Food, wine, and its makings we shared with friends; I left any long skirts I'd made by hand, I wouldn't need them in England. We said *Good Bye* to our second families and friends who had shown such kindness to us and headed north across the Mediterranean Sea and Europe to London.

In the village of Crowthorn, Surrey, Terry had rented us a five-bedroom Charles Church house with white pillars on either side of the front entrance and a tiny garden; the man of the family next door drove a red Ferrari to work.

But since my preference was to have a small house and large garden, I broke the lease as soon as I was able to. In the meantime Roger and I began living there on our own. Terry disappeared. That's when I seriously started to consider reneging on the vow I had taken so seriously: till death-do-us-part. A huge challenge and the most difficult decision I would ever have to make until eventually realizing there was no alternative: Terry had used the past tense, our relationship was over.

Relieved to be back in England but devastated by the strange turn of events I was trying hard to be a responsible mother, supporting Roger as changes to both our lives became more apparent. To keep busy, I sewed name labels onto all of Rogers school uniform parts: grey flannel long-sleeved shirts, navy pullovers with red collars, short grey woolen pants, long grey socks, and school ties. He was a day pupil, not a boarder and from the little bungalow I found to rent, he could safely walk to school through a grassy, rhododendron filled park.

My first meeting with a lawyer went nowhere. She told me to return when I was absolutely sure it was what I wanted to do. On my second visit, having accepted my inevitable new reality, she agreed the time had come to use her authority to dissolve my marriage.

Clearing the Path

Having a tiny car, my family and old friends close by, and employment at the local children's clinic at Frimley, helped me to settle down. By finding a field with a path around it to run on and learning how to bowl a cricket ball to Roger after school, I was able to tuck these memories away and begin to let go of my remarkable past.

Oh, TO be in England
Now that April's there,
And whoever wakes in England
Sees, some morning, unaware,
That the lowest boughs and the brushwood sheaf
Round the elm-tree bole are in tiny leaf,
While the chaffinch sings on the orchard bough
In England—now!
~ Robert Browning

EPILOGUE

My Backpack Heart

Even as a child, I loved to get in the car and go.

Anywhere.

In my twelfth year, Sylvia, my mother, brother Peter and I had a great adventure traveling on the ocean liner *Franconia*, floating from Liverpool in UK to *Québec* City in Canada to join Joseph, my father to start new lives in *Montréal*. On the ship for five days, as Sylvia relaxed in a deckchair with a book, her feet up and a cup of tea within reach, Peter and I enjoyed absolute freedom and fun.

I wasn't a novice traveler when Terry entered my life, I'd visited most of the western European countries on my summer holidays once I'd started working. But opportunities exploded when we started living together, and I was suddenly making long flights to places I'd only dreamt about.

There was, however, a master planner of sorts at work behind the scenes, orchestrating where Terry lived, traveled, and worked. The CIA. Because he had signed up the day before I met him on the ferry, it was a hidden part of his life for as long as I knew him. Recently, the CIA has softened a little by officially having family days; get togethers for socializing and support, even as it continues to protect its employees with secrecy, but in the1960s it was a totally secret organization. Which explained why I was trained not to ask questions; Terry couldn't tell me why he was in the Congo or Nigeria or Laos or what he was doing in those countries. He had to lie about being in Northern Norway too and possibly other countries I haven't dug into. Call-Me-Geoff-Gould in Montreal; someone in Maine; Washington D.C.; and New York City were all his CIA controllers.

Not only secrets but lies became necessary for Terry to use to conceal his double identity, and that habit of lying grew into a pervasive reality until all I knew were lies. When I learned the truth in 2011 by reading Michael Hingston's *Rengade Hero*, Terry's biography, I was traumatized. I felt I'd been manipulated and used. It took a year of saying Ho'opono pono, the Hawaiian prayer of Letting Go: 'I love you, I'm sorry, Please forgive me, Thank you', to forgive him and end my depression. Now I understand how in the early days, he had no choice but to distort the truth. His lies were often clever, for example, when I left him in Northern Norway to live in Australia, he told me he would be flying search and rescue missions. I accepted that. But in reality he was monitoring Russian Naval operations. Not a big deal, but not the truth.

The 1960s were times of incredible and complicated unrest across Africa and Asia when many countries were suddenly thrown into independence. Struggles for power and control, competition for allegiances and alliances burst into action, the CIA's difficult role was to fiercely defend America's political interests. Being recruited by the CIA as a contract provider (mercenary) suited Terry because he was able to do good works while also being immersed in the turmoil. Hingston, in the preface to his biography, describes Terry's: 'engaging personality which binds people to his larger-than-life character of a gentleman warrior and also the Renegade Hero.' Both of which he was. He died in 2015.

Today in 2025, the Democratic Republic of Congo, still a vast repository of precious minerals now needed more than ever for the manufacturing of high-tech devices, remains devastated by enormous and crippling poverty and corruption. Biafra continues struggling to establish the independence it fought for from 1967 to 1970 when two million Igbo tribal people were brutally murdered. In contrast, Laos, with its amazing beauty, welcomes tourists now, its people applauded for their generosity and friendliness. Only one severe CIA warning remains to remind visitors to beware of unexploded ordnance continuing to litter the ground where the most fierce battles were fought between Laotian and North Vietnamese (communist) troops while we were there in 1969.

Roger (Peet), after growing up in South Africa, Norway, Australia, Saudi Arabia, England, and America, chose Portland, Oregon, as his home. He graduated with a degree in Humanities from Oberlin College in Ohio and has developed a deep interest in Africa, especially in the Democratic Republic of Congo, a country he's visited several times, most recently to do research in Katanga Province for his book *Shinkwelobwe*. As an artist, he is using his inspiration and skills to protect the planet and its people. Find more about him on his website: justseeds.org

In addition to all the traveling I did in Africa, Europe and Indonesia, I've also done plenty in Canada and Australia, and in America with my husband Mark and the dogs. When problems arise, I continue to turn to the calming influence of Rouen Cathedral's rose window with its rainbow of colour streaming through the dust motes.

The old excitements don't interest me now. I was happy to settle down with Mark in 1987 in the lee of a mountain, north of Tucson Arizona, where, for twenty years, I worked on the Tohono O'dham Nation, each visit an opportunity for adventure. Now we have a garden to care for and congenial neighbours, and a series of wonderful dogs rescued from the Navajo Nation. Our travels are to be with family and friends and to spend time at our 400-year-old home in the south of France.

Over the past many years these stories have filtered through my thoughts as I've sat back from my computer and looked to the distant western horizon through the sturdy branches of an old mesquite tree, a cup of tea on my desk and two dogs at my feet.

ACKNOWLEDGMENTS

Here's a hearty shout of gratitude and love, dear Mark. Without the almost daily response to my call: 'Mark, are you busy?' and his subsequent appearance at my computer to assist with an unfathomable computer problem, this book would not have been completed. His gifts of time and expertise; the meals he prepared and the washing he hung on the line, his kind words and helpful gestures are very much appreciated.

For several years I have been fortunate to belong to the Rillito River Writers, a group of enthusiastic readers, writers and authors whose history goes back more than a decade. We meet once a week to critique and support the makings of successful true, nonfiction stories. For me, as a beginner writer, these sessions were and are invaluable and my gratitude reflects their importance. Thank you all, and love.

In September 2023 I received an offer from a retired teacher friend to help me organize and edit what I'd recently written; a relationship that grew to almost daily conversations about stories continuing to spring from my memory. Katie Edleman Bultman put herself at my disposal for the year that followed, using her own experience as an author to guide and support me. Eventually we worked our way through all my earlier stories too. The value of her time and her contributions cannot be quantified; every email, every phone call were precious contributions to this finished product. From my heart, thank you Katie and love.

Over the years, friends and family members all over the world who haven't given up on this project all deserve to be remembered with gratitude. Some have read and made suggestions: Mickey Parent in Phoenix, a critical editor early on and one of my beta readers; Reggie Cantu who took the time to read and offer ideas from his home in Okinawa, Japan; my step brother Don Will in *Québec* insisted that I spell *Montréal* correctly; Leslie Kerr-Edwards in Berkshire UK, who's intuitive reading gave me wise insights. And in Tucson: Eleanor Kohloss and Sally Krusing, Susan Pennington and Phyllis Seltzer, the four members of my first small, no-named writing group, who connected with me after we took Molly McKasson's course in 2014. It was Molly, author and actor in Tucson, who inspired me to start this project after taking her course in memoir writing: *Memory and Beyond-The joy and surprise of sharing a life.* I am indebted to you Molly, and thank you all, with love.

Could I have completed the book without the careful reviewing by my beta readers: Pamela Alexander, Mary

Acknowledgments

Lou Forier, Kathleen Jamsa, Elizabeth Reed, Linda Snow, and Mickey? Thanks to each of you for opening my eyes to new possibilities. A special thank you to Elizabeth for not only editing all the English spelling and punctuation, but answering my questions to the very end. What a generous and clever group you are. With love and sincere gratitude.

Turning a page and seeing your drawing of Sparky is such a surprise. Many thanks Roger for being part of my book by so quickly responding to my last minute request, with lots of love.

It took a tip from Nancy Jewett to connect me with graphic designer Brooke O'Neill who agreed to transform my stories into a book. Brooke's enduring patience is matched by her skill in making quick editing changes. Thank you Nancy and thank you Brooke for every minute of your kind attention, with love.

ABOUT THE AUTHOR

Joan Peet Milner is an old English lady who has been writing this book (standing up), with real enjoyment for the last ten years while letting life intrude in some of its unpredictable ways. She has lived in the USA since 1987. Her profession of occupational therapist kept her busy for 46 years while living and working in: Canada, the UK, Nigeria, South Africa, Norway, Australia, Laos, Kauai USA, Saudi Arabia and Arizona USA where she resides with her scientist husband Mark Gettings and two terrific, rescued dogs.

Picture taken by Claudine Glasner, Portiragnes, France.